THE LYTTELTON
HART-DAVIS
LETTERS

THE LYTTELTON HART-DAVIS LETTERS

Correspondence of George Lyttelton
and Rupert-Hart-Davis
Volume Four 1959

Edited and introduced by
RUPERT HART-DAVIS

Correspondences are like small-clothes
before the invention of suspenders;
it is impossible to keep them up.
SYDNEY SMITH

JOHN MURRAY

Lyttelton Letters
© 1982 Humphrey Lyttelton
Hart-Davis letters and notes
© 1982 Sir Rupert Hart-Davis

First published 1982
by John Murray (Publishers) Ltd
50 Albemarle Street, London WIX 4BD
Printed in Great Britain by
The Pitman Press, Bath

British Library Cataloguing in Publication Data
Lyttelton, George
The Lyttelton Hart-Davis letters
Vol. 4: 1959
1. English letters
I. Title II. Hart-Davis, Rupert
826'.914'08   PR1347
ISBN 0-7195-3941-2

This volume is dedicated
by its editor to
ROGER FULFORD
old and dear friend of both writers
and to the happy memory
of his beloved wife
SIBELL

INTRODUCTION

The delightful people who have read and enjoyed the first three volumes of this correspondence, and written to tell me so, will need no further introductory words from me, but newcomers may like to know how it all began.

In 1926 I had been taught by George at Eton, where he was an outstanding teacher and housemaster. He taught mostly classics but in my last year he had started an English course, and it was then that I fell under the spell of his infectious enthusiasm for literature. After I left Eton our ways parted. George taught for a further twenty years before retiring to Suffolk. We met again in 1949 and thereafter saw and wrote to each other occasionally, but the origin of this correspondence was a dinner-party in 1955 during which George complained that no one wrote to him in Suffolk and I accepted his challenge.

To avoid repetitive footnotes I should say that Comfort was my wife; Bridget, Duff, and Adam my children. Ruth Simon had been my beloved prop and stay since 1946.

As before, in the first letters I have retained the opening and signature, which are afterwards omitted, since they are almost always the same: any variation is printed. Similarly I have given our full home addresses in the first two letters and then abbreviated them. From Monday to Friday I lived in a flat above my publishing office at 36 Soho Square. At the beginning of this volume George was almost seventy-six and I was fifty-one.

RUPERT HART-DAVIS

Marske-in-Swaledale
November 1981

4 January 1959

My dear George

It is past eleven p.m. There is snow outside. Russian projectiles are 'orbiting' in a sinister way round every heavenly body. I am behindhand with everything. Our cricketers are a laughing-stock. Our Foreign Secretary has lost his tonsils. There is no health in us.

Your Christmas visit was a joy, though I was much concerned for Pamela. It was heroic of her to come at all, bless her. I saw Diana and Alexander[1] at Philip Astley's memorial service. I am so sad for Joan and the little boy: they were a very happy family, and Philip adored the child.

So glad you're enjoying those Cardus pieces: all my solicitude in cutting out and sticking in, more than twenty years ago, is now amply rewarded. Would that we had Gubby Allen and other 'good Free Forester stuff' in Australia now! I should certainly bring in Trueman, Swetman and Dexter—and cable to that oily Archbishop, asking for a special dispensation by which D. Sheppard could be despatched by rocket.

I am halfway through a borrowed copy of *Lolita* and must finish by Wednesday, when the Herbert Committee meets to consider it and Mr R. A. Butler.[2] I fear that between the two of them our poor old Bill may founder. So far I should say *Lolita*'s literary value was negligible, and its pornographic level high. It is about *nothing* but a middle-aged man's lust for a twelve-year old girl (who had already lost her virginity to the farmer's boy and is quite ready for her elderly lover). No detail is omitted, all told with relish, and in so far as the book

[1] George's daughter and son-in-law.
[2] Under the auspices of the Society of Authors A.P. (Sir Alan) Herbert had organised a committee to draft a suggested Bill to improve the law on Obscenity. R.A. Butler was Home Secretary.

might well suggest to children that sex begins at eleven, I think it should not appear. Did you see that rhyme in one of the weeklies?

> Goldilocks, Goldilocks, wilt thou be mine,
> Although I am ninety, and thou art but nine.

Robert Graves I have known slightly, on and off, for many years. Not an attractive personality. Some of his poems are very good: most of his voluminous prose I haven't read, but sensible people have spoken well of *I Claudius* and others of his historical works. Poets can never live on their poetry, and if they are unwilling to work except with the pen, they are forced to try some sort of prose—Masefield adventure stories for boys and others, the Sitwells all sorts of travel and *belles lettres*, and so on. Graves has tried most things, and generally earned a good living thereby.

I have just realised that perhaps this will reach you on your birthday. Very many happy returns, and may your seventy-seventh year be blessed. As a child you must have missed many presents by your birthday's proximity to your Saviour's. My Bridget's is on the 13th and she seldom gets much, poor lamb.

On Tuesday I am going to resume my plan of getting up at 6.30 and devoting an hour to Oscar before my bath. Without some such pressure the great mass of typescript will never get to the printer, and I am fast forgetting all I ever knew about the subject.

You will soon be getting the first of my 1959 books, which appear on January 30: altogether twenty-four books are due to appear between now and the end of June—too many for my peace of mind.

Today we drove to the Cotswolds to lunch with Comfort's stepmother. Blue skies, bright sun, beauty all the way—and now the wireless warns of fog and frost.

Adam was much taken with you, and I think was much flattered at being allowed a brief *tête-à-tête* with the great man.

Yours ever
Rupert

8 January 1959

My dear Rupert

'Behindhand with everything' is the kind of message found pinned to the coat of a suicide. *Don't do it*—or perhaps at Xmas it is nearly universal. I should be too, but luckily for all concerned I am on the shelf—or almost, as I have at least a month of exceptionally tedious and exacting work, co-ordinating the papers and marking of nine separate boards, and stating what marks the board I am on (Oxford and Cambridge) would have given. We, let me tell you, are the only remotely civilised examiners, i.e. we do *not* think that the object of reading *Macbeth* or Tennyson is solely to acquire two or three hundred isolated *facts*. All the others do, and their instructions to examiners cover five closely typed pages, the reading of which I find literally nauseating, and when pedants like me say 'literally' they mean 'literally'.

We go back to Grundisburgh to-morrow, and I *know* our journey will be in snow and/or over ice. *Marquez mes mots.* Why does one find every winter fouler than the last? And how often the *laudator temporis acti* is right. Perhaps not for wage-earners, though they don't seem all that happy. We get back to Faust, who could never be got to admit contentment whatever they gave him. And you remember the shoe-black passage in *Sartor*.[1] Did you, by the way, notice how *one* of the

[1] 'Will the whole Finance Ministers and Upholsterers and Confectioners of modern Europe undertake, in joint-stock company, to make one Shoeblack HAPPY? They cannot accomplish it, above an hour or two: for the Shoeblack also has a Soul quite other than his Stomach; and would require, if you consider it, for his permanent satisfaction and saturation, simply this allotment, no more, and no less: *God's infinite Universe altogether to himself,* therein to enjoy infinitely, and fill every wish as fast as it rose. Oceans of Hochheimer, a Throat like that of Ophiuchus: speak not of them; to the infinite Shoeblack they are as nothing. No sooner is your ocean filled, than he grumbles that it might have been of better vintage. Try him with half of a Universe, of an Omnipotence, he sets to quarrelling with the proprietor of the other half, and declares himself the most maltreated of men. Always there is a black spot in our sunshine: it is even, as I said, the *Shadow of Ourselves.*'

(Carlyle, *Sartor Resartus*, book 2, chapter ix)

3

two possible theories about how the world began (in the final Reith lecture), i.e. that there is *no* beginning or end, takes us straight to Vaughan's:

> I saw Eternity the other night
> Like a great ring of pure and endless light.

Science limps after the poets for all the massive conceit with which it stiffens its votaries.

Pamela was herself again after twenty-six hours. She would have cried off any other lunch, though unlike so many wives she is not of the 'crying-off' kind. And my daughter Helena and her man Peter Lawrence empower me to urge you to call on them when you come to see Adam. I want you to meet all my daughters, because I think you would like them and I know they would like you. Adam is about a year junior to Aubrey Lawrence and they haven't really met. But Aubrey has a not very clear-cut tale of Adam always failing in construe up to Colquhoun and then getting a Distinction in Trials. The best kind of score *me judice*.

How right you are about birthdays in January. A pencil left over from Xmas, or a small bottle of scent, if you please, are about all one can expect. How did you remember mine? I was born three days after Lord Attlee and no doubt a star danced that week.

Adam was entirely easy to talk to—how should his father's son not be? I don't think I often find Wilde's advice very useful. 'Talk to all women as if you were in love with them, and all men as if bored.' Or have I got it wrong?

I have to-day had a letter from him you call 'that oily Archbishop'. I know him only as a first-rate Chairman and a genial chap. He does laugh a good deal and press photographers always catch him at the zenith of a guffaw, all molars and uvula. A pity. Did Archbishop Laud ever smile? Not that he had much to smile at.

I am coming to the Lit. Soc. on Tuesday and will be straining at your doorbell round about 6. Will your lovely Ruth be there? *Hoffentlich!* Jonah is coming; I have just had a good letter from him—from Alnwick where they have had a week of blue skies and sun, which is quite another pair of shoes from the Thames Valley or Cambridge.

Yours ever
G.W.L.

I am most distressed by Elisabeth Beerbohm's death. She was angelic to me, and one side of her sharply divided nature was warm and cherishing. Certainly she made Max's last five years a paradise for him, but at his death her occupation was gone, and I fear she has been lonely and miserable ever since. Lately she seemed to withdraw more and more into herself, clutching Max and all his works to her, so that it became almost impossible to make any business arrangement with her. Poor darling, I grieve for her, and for her macabre end. Apparently the doctor says she must have died instantly—from a heart attack in her bath—but wasn't found for something like a week!

Goodness knows what will now happen to all the Maxiana, the copyrights etc. On Monday I shall ring up Max's lawyers and find out whether they have Elisabeth's will. As I think I told you, I have long had in mind as many as five or six more Max books, which may now become possible if there are reasonable executors.[1] Today I rang up S.C. Roberts, and he is writing something about Elisabeth for Monday's *Times*.

I wonder what sort of journey home you had. Here there is snow everywhere, but the roads are mainly clear. The cold is bitter and I hug the library fire. Unfortunately at midnight I have to drive to Henley to fetch Adam and some young friends from a dance: the friends have to be distributed all round the countryside.

I love to think that Henry Vaughan was three centuries ahead of the Reith lecturer. What or who do you imagine T.S.E. is foreshadowing in like manner?

I had a charming note from the P.M.,[2] saying that he hasn't been to the Lit. Soc. for years, sees no likelihood of coming, and suggests resigning. Tommy proposes to make him an honorary member, which will create a vacancy and start up the cumbersome electoral machinery next autumn. I think I shall put up Roy Jenkins, the Labour M.P. who wrote the Dilke book, if I can find a seconder. He's very nice, intelligent and friendly.

[1] So far I have produced only five: *Letters to Reggie Turner* (1964), *More Theatres* (1969), *Last Theatres* (1970), *A Peep into the Past and other prose pieces* (1972), and *A Catalogue of the Caricatures* (1972).

[2] Harold Macmillan.

5

Adam, believe it or not, is *making* a wireless set out of a thousand particles of metal! I am astounded that a child of mine should be capable of doing such a thing: my own mechanical skill *just* enables me to switch a set on and off. But I suppose it's no more extraordinary than that *your* son should be the world's leading jazz trumpeter. Certainly the inborn belief that one's children will be recognisable chips off the old block dies hard.

I am in the middle of reading a huge biography of the American dramatist Eugene O'Neill, which has been offered to me. It's extremely interesting, but so long that it will probably have to be priced beyond all sales. It is called *The Curse of the Misbegotten*.

On Friday I slogged out to Putney to lunch with Arthur Ransome and his wife. A.R. was in bed with a bad back, and after lunch we gathered round his bed with a nice young man called John Bell (my co-executor) while Arthur read his will aloud to us. I hope to goodness he lives for ages: he is seventy-five next week.

I was glad to see the authorities included my three candidates in this Test team, though so far Dexter hasn't done much to justify himself.

You will be eagerly awaited at six on Tuesday. The house is full of painters, so your difficulties in gaining admittance will be greater than ever.

I am truly in despair about Oscar: he was so nearly finished last September, and now he slips steadily backward, as other tasks accumulate and my memory softens like melting butter. One difficulty is that this final stage can be completed only in Soho Square, where all the reference and other relevant books are housed.

Now I must return to *The Misbegotten* until it's time to fetch the children: the house never felt warmer.

15 January 1959   *Grundisburgh*

There is nothing new to say about the Lit. Soc. evening, any more than there is about our creation, preservation and all the blessings of this life, which the clergy tell us we ought to give thanks for every day. Your patience—haven't I reason to know it?—is great, but I suppose falls short of the divine, and if I said all I think about you and Ruth and the repast and the company on those celestial Tuesdays, you couldn't help being bored. The hour beforehand in your room sends me to the gathering as mellow as Eric Linklater, but from a different cause; as Arnold Bennett puts it somewhere 'not intoxicated but inclined to take a much more favourable view of the world than it really deserves'. I don't quote accurately but you see the gist.

I was in a good environment—the President, Ivor Brown, and Wheeler-Bennett, whose reception of stories about Hitler and Co which he had been familiar with for years was mere perfection—and I *never* exaggerate. Tommy Lascelles is full of flavour and quality; the only drawback to him is that he will depart so early, and Tim takes him, and I accompany them, Diana living only a hundred yards away. And what a succulent party I left at the end of the table, preparing like the Doctor to fold your hands and have your talk out, R.H-D. especially seeing through all things with his half-shut eyes, as Pope rather optimistically said coffee made the politician do.[1]

Did I tell you that Ivor B, bless him, is going to give away the prizes at the Abbey School on June 5? It is a great weight off my mind. I wrote to seven people without success. What an ass I was not to think of I.B. before; but the luck evens out in the end, as I really think he is the best of the bunch, and I am pretty sure they know it at the Abbey.

I become more like Mr Pooter every day. Believe it or not, we had nearly got to Tommy Lascelles's dwelling when I remembered I had left my bag in the porter's lodge at the Garrick, and the celestial Tim took me back without a murmur.

I returned home this morning—dense fog up to Witham, and then bright sunshine. But the damnable cold has come back, and every grain of the snow that fell last Friday is still there and makes the lawn look like somebody's boothole. Did Peter F. motor home last night? The genial blend of fog and ice has something Dantesque about it.

I see the Russians promise us several men on the moon in a few years' time and some even on Jupiter. That planet they tell me is almost as hot as the sun, so I think Khrusch and Co must be a little optimistic. Anyway I hope they all go there and find they have left

[1] *The Rape of the Lock*, Canto IV.

their refrigerators behind. The moon and its minerals are shortly to be 'exploited'. *Homo sapiens* is a stuffy little fellow, don't you think?

I am expecting great fun with Havelock Ellis,[1] moving about in surely a very strange world. E.g. on pp 20, 21 I somehow miss the full beauty that H.E. sees in all that maternal micturition. And yet he *was* a Victorian. But the necessary adjustments in the point of view would not have been easy for the Worcestershire mind in the mid-nineties.

I have not yet heard what happened today at Sydney, but I felt very contemptuous at breakfast, on reading that as soon as May and Cowdrey struck, Benaud shut the game up for a draw. I simply don't recognise that as the way to play cricket, and can't remember any players before Hutton thinking it was. It is largely the fault of the cricket journalists that everything has got so distorted. I don't yet (3.30 p.m. Thursday) know yesterday's score. May has that mark of the great batsman, of making runs when he is out of form and touch. C.B. Fry's view was that 'we can all make runs when we are fit and seeing the ball', but Ranji could get a hundred v. Briggs and Mold on a lively wicket, when suffering from 'bronchitis, indigestion and *corns*' (a nice anticlimax)—which of course I have told you before, but you *may* have forgotten.

I see my cousin Molly Stanley is dead—one of those really staggering heroines. Fifty years ago she was permanently paralysed below the waist by a hunting accident (her first remark when she became conscious was 'Do take my foot away from my neck, it looks so silly'). She survived, crippled, for half a century, had a family and was never depressed or impatient or out of pain. There must be *something* after death for human beings like that.

P.S. Your Ruth is a lovely thing—body, mind and spirit, and if you or she think that is cheek on my part I can't help it. I had to say it; one must recognise and hail really fine things when one meets them: so there (second time).

---

[1] The biography by Arthur Calder-Marshall.

Yesterday evening, just after the thaw set in, I was summoned by loud cries to the nursery, where Adam, shining with pride, switched on his home-made radio, and through the shrill scream of atmospherics we could distinctly make out a prim Third Programme talk on African Art. I am more than ever astounded at the boy's skill. In his spare time he has fixed up a bird-table outside this window, and I have happily wasted time watching blue-tits, robins, wagtails and the bully blackbird. Comfort says if I watched long enough I should see a nut-hatch—but should I know it if I did?

I thought you were in particularly good form last Tuesday, and so did Ruth. I'm not sure I shall repeat your glowing words to her, for fear of turning her head, but they certainly lifted up my heart on a cold manuscript-ridden Saturday morning—bless you.

Tomorrow night, the last of the holidays, I am taking Adam to *Macbeth* at the Old Vic: the last time I saw the play was with Edmund Blunden at Stratford twenty-five years ago, and I'm looking forward to fresh beauties revealed—as they usually are.

On Friday my telephone-girl (who is very pretty but almost half-witted) got my Paddington taxi ten minutes too soon. I was still signing letters, so told her to make love to the driver till I was ready. She asked him in, and on the way to the station he described the scene with true Cockney wit:

'She said: "The boss says I'm to make love to you till he's ready," but I said: "I'm too old for all that. What I used to do all night now takes me all night to do." '

Here he paused, then said musingly:

'I should say she's a simple girl—the sort you could send out for a pint of pigeon's milk.'

Apparently he had called her attention to the fact that some of the new paint in the front office had been put on back to front, and she was duly impressed.

Yesterday I actually managed to put in a couple of hours on poor old Oscar. Apart from completing the notes and writing my introductions, all the numberless corrections have got to be transferred to the top copy of the typescript for the printer. This is comparatively automatic work, requiring no books or preparation, so that one can do it piecemeal. Unfortunately Diana Cooper's and Peter's page-proofs are coming in simultaneously next week, so I shall be busier than ever, especially as I have to make Diana's index.

There still seems to be no trace of Elisabeth Beerbohm's having made a will, so all depends on her sister. Tomorrow I am lunching at the Athenaeum with S.C. Roberts to discuss this and other matters. I believe he is to be the next speaker at the Johnson Club (on March 10): if so we must attend. I hear that Prof. Sutherland resigned after that filthy meal in the Garret, but now the Cheshire Cheese is doing well.

I have been bidden to a feast at King's on March 14 as the Provost's guest, and shall certainly go. It's very nice of him to ask me. I shall probably stay with Humphry House's widow, unless, as seems possible, she is even then having her gall-bladder removed, poor lamb. On March 18 I have promised to address the assembled book-collectors of Manchester: 'it was an insensate step'.

Yesterday I read the whole of a novel which I've just had translated from the French. It's called *The Lion*[1] and I think you'll like it, for most of the characters are wild animals. There's another about Alexander the Great, which I should have read weeks ago—oh dear, where is the time?

All this is while I read two or three detective stories a week (in bed), but I fear my source may soon dry up, since *Time and Tide* is clearly on its last legs. I shall miss this solace after a steady supply for fifteen years. And to think that the vast majority of the world's population never reads a book of any kind! They don't, you know, however much we may kid ourselves. Thank heaven I don't have to be one of them!

23 January 1959   *Grundisburgh*

This really *must* be a scrap and no mistake, as this filthy job of investigating the exam-papers and scripts of other boards is laborious beyond words. As a rival to the business of looking in a dark room for a black hat which isn't there, I confidently put up marking a closely

[1] By Joseph Kessel.

written answer of three sides to a question on a 500-page book which one read over fifty years ago. And what old Pardon[1] once described as 'touching the confines of lunacy' (the actions of the selection committee of 1909) would equally apply to the well-meaning organisers having obliterated all the marks and underlinings of the original examiners (and sometimes a line or two of the answer as well). So I am rather up against it, and they want all the stuff by the end of the month, damn them. I need hardly say that in the paper on the *Midsummer Night's Dream* searching questions are asked about the plot and the characters and none about the poetry, though everyone except an Eng. Lit. examiner knows that 1 and 2 are absurd, and 3 is incomparable. Enough!

The young are marvellous. Adam's radio! Did old Fred Coleridge stimulate that? *He* doesn't know a radio from a rabbit, any more than I do. And I still gnash my teeth over my fatuous ignorance of trees and birds. My old father should have mildly bribed us in the holidays to acquire the elements of country life. Bribery is a very important part of holiday education, but that generation didn't know it.

Oh! these cricketers! strains, fractures, sorenesses, belly-aches (literal and metaphorical) after every match, and nobody knows why. The return of Lindwall is interesting. But the *Times* man was wrong about one thing. He wasn't the fastest: Miller's fast one was quicker. How do I know? Sir Hutton told me—at the same meal at which he said apropos of Ramadhin that it was awkward playing a bowler when you didn't know which way the ball would turn on pitching, but still more awkward when the bowler didn't know either.

That is a very good conversation between your telephone girl and the taximan. We once had a man-cook, retired seaman, who described our half-witted boot-boy as 'put in with the bread and taken out with the cakes'. 'The sort you could send out for a pint of pigeon's milk' is infinitely subtle. Falstaff might have said it.

I was immensely interested in the Havelock Ellis life—but rather strongly nauseated by him. Surely his kind of sexual contact is the one most hated by women, and didn't I once read a French novel all about that? I was interested to see that Inge greatly admired him but couldn't do with his most famous work—wouldn't have it in his

[1] Sydney Pardon, writer on cricket.

house in fact. H.E.'s marriage is an extraordinary story, crammed with oddity and a good deal of heroism. He is one of those—rather like old Carlyle—whose defects one thinks one could easily avoid and whose virtues one couldn't get within a mile of. They were a rum lot —James Hinton, a most sinister man; and Olive Schreiner!

You will like Noel Annan. Give him my regards. I met him at the Founder's feast two years ago. The youngest head of a college that ever was; I realised at the dinner that he might easily have been in my house—awful! (Do you know the right collective noun—e.g. a pride of lions—for heads of colleges? *A lack of principals*; and for wing-commanders? *A flush of W.C.s.* Neither of them mine.) I look forward to *The Lion*. (How, pray, am I henceforth to clothe my naked greed in decent garb, now that you have exposed my camouflage to the delight and gentle mockery of Ruth?)

I have just re-read *Jane Eyre, Oliver Twist, The Warden* and *Cranford.* I will *not* read *Hard Times* or *Redgauntlet.*

26 January 1959   *Bromsden Farm*

We are a preoccupied pair: you with your examination-papers, and I with a streaming, stupefying cold which fell upon me yesterday morning and is still in full flow. I can keep only one eye open at a time, my head feels like cotton wool, and I fear your ration of correspondence this week will be both exiguous and dreary. After my seven-years' immunity from colds this one (my second of the winter) finds me outraged and full of self-pity—the least attractive, surely, of all attitudes.

No nuthatches have come to cheer me, unless my rheumy eyes mistook them for sparrows. All the same, the bird-table is a great delight.

Adam is back at Eton, with his wireless, watching the floods creeping up South Meadow and wondering how far they will have to get before the whole Coleridge contingent is sent home. Did that ever happen in your day? I remember devoutly praying that it would in mine.

Adam and I both hugely enjoyed the Old Vic *Macbeth*. An actor called Michael Hordern played Macbeth better than I have ever seen him played before (Gielgud was a disaster in the part), the others were adequate, the production was good, and every one of the matchless words clearly audible. Beatrix Lehmann's Lady Macbeth was not a success, except in the sleep-walking scene which she did beautifully. Earlier she trembled on the edge of comic parody, but it's a terribly difficult part for any actress.

The Havelock Ellis book (out next Friday) looks like getting a lot of reviews, and perhaps sales as well. Have you read *To be Young*[1] (which I should have sent you)? Raymond Mortimer rang up to say he likes it enormously and will review it next Sunday. I have just read Peter's book for the *fourth* time (the final proofs) and still think it extremely good and interesting. He and Tommy are having a splendid correspondence about the Lit. Soc.'s electoral procedure. Tommy says he welcomes new members he didn't know before: 'I prefer the buggers I don't know to those I do.' The debate continues.

As you may have seen, our poor old Obscenity Bill got its second reading (for the second time) on Friday, and A.P. Herbert has retired from East Harrow.[2] This was settled at a meeting of the Herbert Committee in the Savile Club on Friday afternoon. We have now pretty well reached the limit of compromise, and if in Committee the Government try to emasculate the Bill further, we shall withdraw it and start again. That idiotic and gratuitous letter in *The Times* about *Lolita* on the very day the Bill was coming up is considered deliberate sabotage, particularly since two of the signatories are on the main Herbert Committee, and a few days earlier had agreed that for the moment the less said about *Lolita* the better.

A.P.H. was in splendid form on Friday, and when I got home I took down his *Misleading Cases* (untouched these many years) and was delighted to find how amusing and well written they are. Clearly one shouldn't read the book straight through, but I recommend one or two taken at bedtime.

I will allow you to leave *Hard Times* on the shelf, but I beg you to reconsider your harsh decision about *Redgauntlet*. It is almost my

---

[1] By Mary Lutyens.

[2] Where he had threatened to stand as an Independent at a by-election and, if elected, to bulldoze his own Obscenity Bill through the House, as he had his Divorce Bill.

favourite of all that noble band, and I think perhaps you have forgotten it. Or have you only an edition in very small print? If so I shall be tempted to forget my principles and lend you my first edition, in which the words on each page are so few and so well set out that they practically read themselves. The early nineteenth century was the peak-time for novel-printing, and most later novelists (e.g. Dickens and Thackeray) suffered from huge, crowded, eye-straining pages. The only things worse than too-long lines are very short ones printed in double-column like a newspaper. Nowadays the fearful cost of paper and everything else compels one to get as many words into each page as one decently can.

Comfort has just brought me some hot whisky-and-lemon, which, combined with the pleasure of writing to you, seems to have staunched my cold for the moment. Luckily I have no engagements till Tuesday, when I lunch with the Governor of Lloyd's, an old army friend.

30 January 1959 *Grundisburgh*

> He nothing common did or mean
> Upon that memorable scene,
> But with his keener eye
> The axe's edge did try.[1]

No doubt you have already drunk to the memory of the royal martyr?

I am very sorry about that cold, and so is Pamela, but she always maintains that the more streaming, the sooner gone. So I am in hopes that when you get this your nose will be as quiescent, your eye as dry and clear, and your voice as bell-like as they normally are. I recognise and hail the note of outrage in your reporting on it, because I too never get a cold and protest to high heaven when I do. But according to our local chemist, they are on the point of discovering the preventative, in fact he thinks *he* has. He is not wholly unlike Uncle Ponderevo in *Tono-Bungay*.[2]

[1] Andrew Marvell, 'An Horatian Ode upon Cromwell's return from Ireland'. King Charles I was beheaded on 30 January 1649.
[2] By H.G. Wells.

14

I fear Adam has watched the anti-cyclone with fading hopes: the floods must be falling visibly. But I fear, in any case, South Lawn is rarely or never flooded—certainly not as soon as Warre House or its neighbour. The unsportsmanlike architect built it on piles, and even in 1947 (when the water to be disposed of was three-and-a-half times greater than in the great flood of 1894) South Lawn, like Satan, stood like a tower 'proudly eminent'. I missed 1894 by one year, but we had fine skating at Evelyn's over the fields and fallows; some old boys skated from Eton to Evelyn's (near Uxbridge). Those were the days.

Macbeth. You make my mouth water. Of course Gielgud wouldn't do; whoever cast him for it must have been a fool. Do you know the enclosed sentence of Masefield's? Anyway you won't mind being reminded of it.

> Let your Macbeth be chosen for the nervy, fiery beauty of his power. He must have tense intelligence, a swift leaping, lovely body, and a voice able to exalt and to blast. Let him not play the earlier scenes like a moody traitor, but like Lucifer, star of the morning. Let him not play the later scenes like a hangman who has taken to drink, but like an angel who has fallen.
>
> [John Masefield, *A Macbeth Production,* 1945]

I like to remember how when Bourchier in the part charged every word, look, movement, with sinister and even appalling significance, C.E. Montague observed that even murder wasn't as serious as all that. As to Lady M., who ever really played her right throughout? I never saw the great Ellen, but I cannot believe she did, for all her magnificence. The first thing she was was *lovable*—surely the last Lady M was? To avoid caricature, hasn't the actress got to do that hardest of all things, viz. *under*play verbally and vocally, and at the same time give an appalling impression of malevolent strength and determination behind every word, and who the devil can do that? Rosalind, late Countess of Carlisle, perhaps.[1] She had no imagination, but then neither had Lady M. (You remember the admirable Bradley on 'What, in our house?')[2] How good to hear that audibility is coming

[1] See note p. 103.
[2] *Shakespearean Tragedy* by A.C. Bradley (1904), p. 369.

15

back to the stage. Just when senescence began to slow my ears, audibility was regarded as 'ham', and how old Agate raged! He, by the way, always maintained that Macbeth was a far harder part than Lear, the blend of murderer and poet being beyond human scope. I wonder.

I look forward to the Havelock reviews. You make no comment on my rather prim reactions, but is it any good pretending one *wasn't* born in January 1883? I expect both you and Ruth must sometimes think me an old granny—as in fact I am when I hear or read emphatic eulogies of the Osbornes, the Amises, the cats on hot tin roofs etc. But you often reassure me by sharing my opinions, and if Ruth's perception is not as swift and winged and straight to the central gold as an arrow, well then mine must be as wide of the target as was the Lord Lieutenant of Worcestershire who opened the County Archery meeting at Hagley in 1890 with a shot which missed the entire target and the protective canvas behind it, and hit a cow in the backside some eighty yards away.

But now for bell, book, and candle, which you were going to get anyway. I read *one* chapter of *Redgauntlet* which answered one of the questions in an exam-paper, thought it excellent and made a note of *R.* for my next bedside book. I had so totally forgotten it that I am not even sure I *did* read it, and I was vaguely classing it with *Castle Dangerous* etc. when I foolishly condemned it to you (G.K. Chesterton: 'We all have a profound and manly dislike for the book we have not read').

To be Young is my next venture (with *Redgauntlet*! I generally have two going at once). It was in your last batch of generosity.

That is a deliciously characteristic remark of Tommy Lascelles, and how well one knows what he means. How pleasant and satisfactory it is that people should be different; they apparently won't be much longer.

Years ago some foul boy borrowed and never returned my *Misleading Cases*. I loved it—as I do *Topsy* as well. His pen is quite unerring in these regions. Is *M.C.* still in print? Or to be found in the Charing Cross Road?

What did I read recently about a scandalous pub in Soho Square where things are done you'd not believe in Soho Square on Xmas eve? You have kept strangely silent about this. Perhaps you are a director.

16

If it isn't one thing it's another. Diana's proofs have so occupied my week-end that it is now past bedtime on Sunday night, and not a line written to you. Nor have I any events to retail. That cold proved to be one of the most virulent I've ever encountered, and I was compelled to spend the first half of last week in bed in the flat, streaming from nose and eyes, unable to read and very sorry for myself. Darling Ruth nursed me so devotedly that she inevitably caught the cold, so when I got up I put her to bed and nursed her. Now we are both quite recovered. All my 'engagements' had to be cancelled, including the luncheon with the Chairman (not Governor, as I said last week) of Lloyd's.

Adam reported every inch of the Eton floods with scientific objectivity—2 ft 6 below the '47 mark, three yards from Fred's boys'-entrance, his garden-seats floating away, swans on South Meadow. He has 'done something fatal' to his wireless, but is confident of its resurrection. He has been made captain of the house Junior League soccer side (some new-fangled innovation) and since they won their first match 11–0 his hopes are high. I sent him that *admirable* bit of Masefield. I agree with every word of it, and the actor we saw didn't fall far short of M.'s ideal. When Oscar saw Irving and Ellen Terry at the Lyceum in 1888 he wrote: 'Judging from the banquet, Lady Macbeth seems an economical housekeeper and evidently patronises local industries for her husband's clothes and the servants' liveries, but she takes care to do all her own shopping in Byzantium.' Can't you *see* the whole production?

Neither Ruth nor I ever for a moment think of you as 'an old granny'. On the contrary, we marvel at your easy acceptance of modern lapses and intransigence.

Thank goodness you're weakening about *Redgauntlet,* which I *know* you'll love. *Castle Dangerous* was the pitiable production of a worn-out, dying man.

My books did well to-day—two long leading reviews in each of the two important papers. I'm particularly pleased about *To be Young*: the author is so charming.

I must try and find you a copy of *Misleading Cases.* When I read in

the papers of the gang-wars, stabbings, strip-tease and general de-
bauchery, with which Soho is clearly riddled, I marvel that I have
lived in the heart of it for eight and a half years without a glimpse of
any such activities. I suppose you might say the same about incest and
scoutmastery in Suffolk, which no doubt are reported each week in the
News of the World. To the pure, my dear George, all things are reported.

Six winter aconites are bravely flowering in the garden. Perhaps
spring isn't so far behind. Don't you agree that the *first* flowers of the
year are much the most exciting, surprising one each time? But there
are in fact at least two more hellish months ahead of us. The London
air last week was disgusting, and I was thankful to miss so much of it
by being in bed. I do hope you'll nevertheless be able to get to the
next Lit. Soc. dinner on Tuesday week. Now the iron tongue of midnight has tolled goodness knows what, and I must to bed. Perhaps I'll
have more to tell you next week. Let's hope so!

4 February 1959 (Thomas Carlyle died 4 February 1881) *Grundisburgh*

You shouldn't do it really. The idea of starting your letter to me
after midnight, weak and flat after the worst of colds. How can you
not resent my existence at such a moment? Be *very* careful now; the
east wind is abroad in the land like Bright's angel of death, and there
is that familiar February phenomenon of the thermometer saying the
temperature is 40° and the tips of one's ears and nose saying it is 20°.

I enjoyed *To be Young*, especially the first part, which is wonderfully
vivid, and never flags, though I for one find it very hard to see how
she does it—style or character or both, I suppose. But my sympathies
with these Theosophists are as imperfect as Lamb's with Quakers,
and somehow I can't quite do with Bishop Leadbeater. I forget what
happened in the matter of homo-scandal, of which he apparently got
cleared. But I put it to you that strong suspicions in that province are
nearly always justified. Or was that only in the past? I mean against
men like Helbert of West Downs or 'Sligger'[1] of Balliol, who had
immense influence with the young, there was never a whisper. Perhaps
there would be nowadays. I suppose the oddly frequent allusions to

[1] Nickname of F.F. Urquhart.

water-closetry in Mary L's book merely show she was her father's daughter. I remember him bubbling over with some such anecdote at Provost Quickswood's table. It was *not* a success.

I have had a nice little local *row*! Asked to contribute to a leaving-present for a Woodbridge parson—unwillingly sent cheque for £1—not acknowledged—wrote fortnight after to ask had it arrived—no answer—wrote to protest about discourtesy—organiser offended—and asked didn't I know that cheques need not be acknowledged nowadays—wrote glacially commenting on organisers regarding a contribution to a gift in same light as payment of tradesman's bill. No answer. There isn't one of course, but alas, he has my £1. Bad manners make me positively waspish, nothing much else does. The organiser said he was not in the habit of being discourteous. I ought to have answered as Gussie Fink-Nottle did when old Tom Travers said he had never talked nonsense. 'Then, for a beginner, you do it dashed well.'[1]

How right you are about the year's first flowers. And what about

> The full-throated daffodils
> Our trumpeters in gold
> Call resurrection from the ground
> And bid the year be bold.[2]

I quote this every year. Forgive me. It usually comes in March.

7 February 1959   *Bromsden Farm*

I shall post this tomorrow, to make sure of catching you. Adam reports abortive skating on flooded football-fields, but has now retired with flu, after his side had won their second *soccer* match 23–0. His G.C.E. marks seem to me very good, but perhaps it's just parental pride. Latin 95% and 85%, Greek 78% and 70%, French 81%, Maths 95%, 96%, 88% and 93%, Physics 92% and 83%—and so on, surely Fred should be pleased? Like you, I have never taken much interest in professional soccer, and haven't watched a game since goodness knows when.

[1] P.G. Wodehouse, *Right Ho, Jeeves*, chapter 17.
[2] C. Day-Lewis, *From Feathers to Iron*, section 14.

So glad you enjoyed *To be Young*: it continues to receive excellent reviews, and the author is transported with joy. How can any sane person have taken those preposterous Theosophists seriously? Clearly Mrs Besant had a terrific personality, but Leadbeater and the rest were appalling. I know nothing of Helbert of West Downs, but Sligger I knew at Balliol and very much disliked. A purring old doctored tom-cat, who gave lemonade-parties at which he stroked the knees of rugger-blues—ugh! I've never seen a more completely homosexual man, though for all I know he may have sublimated his horrid passion with mountaineering and hair-shirts.

Yesterday Jonah brought me the typescript of his new book, which is delightfully entitled *I Forgot to Tell You*. I must read it before Monday. Also a chunk of the first volume of Stephen Potter's autobiography, which, like all his manuscripts, is a mass of dirty bits of paper, vilely typed, corrected in illegible biro, episodic and half-revised. My patience with authors diminishes rapidly.

I loved hearing of your row about the parson's leaving-present: if you'd been a little quicker you could have stopped your cheque. As I have often said to you before, and shall often say again, the older I get, the more important do good manners seem to me.

Later. I've now read Jonah's first fifty pages—with great pleasure. The book consists of a number of chapters, unconnected one with another, each containing a reminiscence which he forgot to include in his three previous volumes. Without their previous publication and success, this would scarcely stand on its own, but as a pendant and epilogue it should do well. I am touching up his spelling, punctuation, and occasionally grammar, as I go along—which necessarily slows me up. I never cease to wonder at the inability of so many otherwise-intelligent people to spell, remember the look of words and names, or look them up.

A neighbour who came to lunch today aroused my envy by telling me that her bird-table (a mile from here) is regularly visited by cross-bills! Have you ever seen one? She says they like pine-needles, which she has nearby and I lack. I must import some.

As the weeks pass and Oscar lies unfinished, I despair of ever completing the task. It begins to look as though R's and my Yorkshire holiday in June will have to be devoted to the job. Last June we expected to be correcting the proofs in a year's time! The publishing business and my other London activities have grown to be so multifarious that I have *no* spare time left.

12 February 1959 (birthday of Abraham Lincoln)   *Grundisburgh*

After good-nighting you, Roger, Betjeman and I drifted into a neighbouring pub where hoi polloi were in force. We were the only men wearing hats and they came in for a good deal of derision—J.B's rightly, for it was almost non-existent in depth, and sat on the noble brow like the crest of a waxwing (do you have them in Oxon? One appeared in the garden here a week ago). But a sozzled Canadian made a dead set at me, on the ground mainly that I didn't know the right way of wearing a Hamburg, as he called it. So I had to ask him to show me the right way. He put it on and was not the first man to find that his head went very little of the way towards filling it. He returned it, hiccuping that I had the largest head not only in England but in France too. It was all very inconsequential and odd. Tommy Lascelles would not have been amused.

Suffolk is silent and windless and drab under a sky of apparently eternal sepia. There were two men in my carriage who talked a little rugger-shop. I think they were ex-blues. I felt no urge to stroke their knees even if they hadn't been heavily ulstered. There was also a very plain elderly lady who smeared and powdered herself *twice* between Liverpool Street and Colchester. At the end she gazed long at her handiwork in her glass and, like the Creator at the end of the sixth day, saw that it was good. I could have told her different, as Sir W. Robertson used to say to the cabinet.

Adam's soccer side is surely making history. Are you sure it isn't rugger? I see Eton is taking the game very seriously and shouldn't wonder if the Field Game is on its way out, but like cricket—and of course Charles II—will probably be an unconscionable time a-dying. Adam's G.C.E. marks are quite outstanding—not a weak spot anywhere. I suppose he is doomed to science—the first leading scientist perhaps to blend science and the arts.

Crossbills are unknown to me (not that that is odd) but also I believe unknown in Suffolk. Starlings are the devil; I was pleased to read that for some forgotten reason hundreds or even thousands of them died recently. Pigeons are a foul nuisance too in these parts. Do you see eye to eye with those who say *all* things are sent for our good? Our rector is one of them. H.G. Wells has a fine indictment of this optimism in *The Undying Fire*. He makes it very hard to maintain one's affection for the liver-fluke, which, in the delicious words of Mrs Cadogan[1], 'plays tallywack and tandem' with one's liver.

Pamela is sitting at the rector's feet listening to his lenten address —not because she wants to, but to swell his meagre audience. Last night she attended the Youth Club, merely because the good woman who runs it said no adult ever came. To-morrow we both go to hear a lecture on leprosy for a more mundane reason, viz. I have a morbid interest in leprosy (another of God's ultimate blessings?) ever since reading about Damien. His life—with a good deal of skipping and editing, made a good Sunday Private—with of course Stevenson's famous outburst of fury to end with. Do you remember that awful word of his describing what it must have been like living with lepers and, whenever there was a knock at the door, not knowing what kind of 'butt-end' of humanity would enter?[2]

I must go to bed and start on *Redgauntlet*. I must also tell you that on re-reading your last it is clear that your sentence about Sligger will have to go in my book. Posterity shall not be deprived of 'a purring old doctored tom-cat' down to 'mountaineering and hair-shirts'. Dons and beaks and scoutmasters are always suspect unless—and this is the wry and rather dreadful truth—they deliberately restrict their *good* feelings for youth from developing to the full—they go too near the edge to escape the prurient insinuations which we all enjoy harbouring.

[1] The housekeeper in *The Experiences of an Irish R.M.* by E.Œ. Somerville and Martin Ross (1899).

[2] Father Joseph Damien, a Belgian missionary (1840–1889), spent his last sixteen years tending the lepers on Molokai Island in the South Pacific and eventually died of leprosy. Robert Louis Stevenson's scathing Open Letter to a Presbyterian clergyman who had traduced Damien's memory was published in 1890.

Your unedifying visit to the pub reminds me of the Chinese pro-
verb: 'The Dragon in Shallow Waters became the Butt of Shrimps.'
Changing Hamburg hats with drunken Canadians indeed! What
would your fellow-examiners say? In future I shall have to make sure
that Tim drives you straight home, and no larking about! I walked
back to Soho Square through the serried ranks of tarts shrilly discussing Mr Butler, Sir John Wolfenden and the musical glasses. Either
because of them, or because I'm not used to so much wine and company, I scarcely slept at all that night. The most tiresome thing about
insomnia is that if one *knew* one was going to be awake for three hours,
one could get up and do three hours' useful work. As it is, one tosses
and turns, hoping to drop off again, neither asleep or awake. However,
it doesn't often happen to me nowadays, thank heaven.

How was your lecture on leprosy? In my salad-days I took part in
a three-hour variety performance at the leper colony in Essex (the
only one in this country, I believe). We had fully rehearsed a three-act
comedy (two men, two women) called *The Mollusc,* but at the last
minute the mother of one of the girls refused to let her go, for fear of
catching leprosy. So we collected another couple of chaps (including a
pianist) and did our best. We were housed and fed (for the evening)
in a bungalow so drenched with disinfectant that one could scarcely
get one's breath, and we performed in a decent-sized hall with a
proper stage at one end. If our planned programme had gone through
we should have been protected from seeing our audience by foot-
lights. As it was, all the lights were on, and although it was encouraging to see the lepers' pleasure, their appearance was most distressing.
I remember in particular a grizzled old sea-captain and a little girl of
nine or so. My dear friend Charlie Marford, the Cockney actor who
had arranged the whole thing, was indefatigable and full of resource.
We acted scenes from Shakespeare (Dogberry and the Watch, Shylock
and Tubal etc), sang songs, went through the motions of dancing, and
racked our brains for other stunts. I read aloud the whole of Oscar's
story 'The Happy Prince', and Charlie did lightning sketches of don-
keys which, when turned upside down, proved to be caricatures of
Lloyd George. It was all most exhausting, and strangely moving: all

23

those doomed and mutilated people apparently so simply delighted. That was in 1928: nowadays I expect they have television and such diversions.

I can't remember what I wrote last week about the Wilde letters, but it seems to have misled you. 98% of the work is *done*, but I can't send the manuscript to the printer without the final 2%, and that simply can't be done at odd moments. It needs a clear fortnight, with no other work, and all the O.W. reference books (which are at Soho Square) around me. Even if I waited for June in Swaledale, it would mean carting dozens of books, and all the manuscript, along. But how am I to find the time before then? Every evening I spend dining out puts my publishing work further in arrears: it's endlessly tiresome.

I sent Ruth a Valentine on Thursday—the first I have ever dispatched. She was much pleased. She is my prop and joy.

19 February 1959   *Grundisburgh*

How pithy Chinese sayings always are! Geoffrey Madan unearthed a good many, but there was a strong suspicion among his friends that he invented quite a lot of them. I like 'A man with a red nose may not drink, but nobody thinks so' and 'Better the chill blast of winter than the hot breath of a pursuing elephant'.

Insomnia can be the devil. I have had a bout or two, but none since breathing the narcotic air of Suffolk. I remember finding Horder's counsel good, viz 'One can do with very little sleep. Lie quite still and don't toss about or worry; then you will get plenty of rest: it's worry that does the harm'. Nice and dull and obvious and hard to follow, like all the best advice.

The leprosy lecture was dreadfully tame—no 'butt-ends' of humanity, only a few men who had a few what looked like water-blisters of the most domestic variety. Practically all the slides were of scenery. There are more flowers and sunshine in Sarawak than in Suffolk. It seems that leprosy is on the point of being 100% curable, though it will always take a goodish time. I am afraid Gehazi leaving Elisha's

24

presence 'a leper white as snow' is mere rhetoric. The whiteness of a leper is like that of a white elephant, i.e. a lot of greyish scruffiness looking like patches of dust. Not for a moment did poor Gehazi resemble the Warre House double cherry-tree in April, which had the whiteness of snow and then some. I should like Housman to have seen it.

Apropos of him the Headmaster of Bromsgrove wants a column on H. for the *Bromsgrovian,* as March 29 is the centenary of H's birth. Oh yes I told you. And the *admirable* John Carter says he will do it—on condition that the Headmaster will lend him the *Bromsgrovian* of 1877 for the Housman exhibition from August to Michaelmas which J.C. is organising. It has some rare early work of H's in it—which I have no doubt the old curmudgeon refused to do anything about subsequently if anyone asked about it. A perfectly fair bargain of J.C.'s I think. I hope there isn't some grim Housmanly embargo on any such transaction at Bromsgrove. But the Headmaster tells me that there is no evidence that H. had the smallest affection for his old school, though I suppose they must have taught him pretty well. Perhaps he was like Osbert Sitwell whose education in *Who's Who* is entered as 'in the holidays from Eton'.

It is delightfully characteristic that you should have entertained lepers in your youth—and from what you say of their appearance, it must have been before sulphonal had been discovered. In about 1904 Downing College (Leavis's) with its lovely grounds and shortage of students, where 'every prospect pleases and only man is vile',[1] was the butt of much crude wit. One term instead of its usual terminal intake of two black men and no other, the rumour went round that *one* white freshman had come. Two days later the rumour was corrected; the white man was really a negro with leprosy. Weren't we mad wags in 1904?

I still haven't got on to *Redgauntlet,* held up recently by the charming Cecilia Ridley—a very good lass.[2] I am glad to see that amid the chorus of praise for Miss Lutyens, Brother Leadbeater gets a poorish press. I hope you share my admiration and liking for old Lincoln,

[1] Bishop Heber (1783–1826), 'From Greenland's Icy Mountains'.
[2] *Cecilia:* the Life and Letters of Cecilia Ridley, 1819–1845, edited by Viscountess Ridley (1958).

25

whose health you drank last week. That delightfully earthy coarseness of his! Only Churchill of our P.M.'s could have defended in the cabinet some unexpectedly large expenditure with 'Gentlemen, you can't manure a ten-acre field with a fart'. Mr Gladstone? *Infandum!* But L. was as good a man as Mr G.

Tell me something brilliant to say about Herrick, on whom I am writing for Dick Routh's Junior National Biography. He wrote over twelve hundred lyrics. Too many, some immensely bad. But then he suddenly produces 'Here a little child I stand, Heaving up my either hand' which is simply and easily delicious. He seems to have paid about as much attention to the civil war etc as Jane Austen did to the Napoleonic. Similarly future editors of *your* letters will comment on your lack of apparent interest in the hydrogen bomb. Very unlike Cicero's letters—and very much less boring.

22 February 1959   *Bromsden Farm*

I go further than you, and assume that *all* 'Chinese proverbs' originated in the western world. I'm particularly fond of 'Ask the young: they know everything.' When I was young I took this literally, and gracefully accepted it as a tribute to the clear-eyed omniscience of youth. Now that I have grown-up children I see that the saying is wholly ironical.

So glad John Carter turned up trumps. I suppose Laurence Housman's death will entail another piece in the *Bromsgrovian*. L.H. was a tiresome old cissy (Hugh Walpole once told me L.H. had got into trouble for picking up a boy in a public lavatory—not, I should have thought, a highly romantic trysting-place), and he made a frightful hash of A.E.H.'s remains. I always think A.E.H. himself was largely to blame: he had the greatest contempt for L.H. and his works, and yet left him to decide what unpublished material should be printed. Most of L.H.'s many books are dim and dated, but some of his little plays have life in them, and in one called *Echo de Paris* he wonderfully re-captured (so responsible witnesses affirm) Oscar's conversation in 1899–1900. I used to see L.H. sometimes when I worked for Cape, who latterly published him.

I can see that you are funking *Redgauntlet*: be brave and jump in: you won't want to come out, I promise you. Yes, Lincoln was a splendid man: I must read more about him. The Gettysburg address is pretty good by any standards, isn't it?

Your saying that my letters are 'very much less boring' than Cicero's, though flattering, is not wholly reassuring. Admittedly there are widely differing degrees of boredom—but I accept the remark as a slip of the biro.

I can't help you with Herrick. Veronica Wedgwood has three good pages on him in her excellent little book *Seventeenth-Century Literature* (O.U.P. 1950), from which I learn that 'during the whole of the eighteenth century he (R.H.) was wholly forgotten and he had to wait for rediscovery until Maitland's edition of his work in 1825.' (If I had published the book I should have made her avoid the juxtaposition of 'whole' and 'wholly', but let that pass.) Which only goes to prove what old Edward Garnett used to say of literary reputation: 'Don't worry: everything finds its own level in the end.' V.W. writes: 'His particular talent, which could so well express the transient sweetness of a summer frolic or the crackling warmth of a winter festival, may speak an *envoi* to the whole [there she is again!] bright gathering of writers who were travelling so fast, with their country, into the bleak season of civil war.' Do what you can with that.

One day I dined with my old (prep-school) friend Wyndham Ketton-Cremer. He is writing a book about Felbrigg, his lovely Norfolk home, and he wants me to publish it for him. It is likely to be his best book and I am pleased.

Adam's soccer side last week won 27–0. He assures me it really is *soccer*. Duff promises to bring a team of stalwart diggers over from Oxford, and Comfort has promised them each three and sixpence an hour—we may be ruined.

Today was *warm* and *sunny*. Comfort gardened herself to a standstill, and I did a little work myself, besides sitting in the sun trying to wield the Sunday papers. Peter walked over and went through his finally revised proofs. His mother-in-law is now pretty well moribund in his house, which is rather a bore for him.

From inscriptions on the Great Wall of China

(1) The Three Good Things:
    (a) Certainty held in Reserve.
    (b) Unexpected Praise from an Artist.
    (c) Discovery of Nobility in Oneself.

(2) The Three Bad Things:
    (a) Unworthiness crowned.
    (b) Unconscious Infraction of the Laws of Behaviour.
    (c) Friendly Condescension of the Imperfectly Educated.

Plausible inventions if spurious?

The omniscience of the young—yes. Old Henry Jackson told us he had heard W.H. Thompson, the Master of Trinity, at a College meeting say to a young Fellow: 'We are none of us infallible, not even the youngest', which if you ever come across you will always find ascribed to Jowett. It puzzles me that W.H.T., the grimmest, and Aldis Wright, the second grimmest of men should both have been great friends of FitzGerald, surely the ungrimmest of men. I like to remember that some spirited undergraduates once pushed a sheep into A.W.'s room at Trinity. The sheep was all against it, and there was a good deal of scuffling before entry was effected. A.W. was sitting on a hard straight-backed chair with his top-hat on (he was said to wear it in bed) and there followed this faultlessly simple dialogue: 'What's this, what's this?' 'A sheep, sir,' and the door banged. Did you know that no smell has such stamina as a sheep's, especially if it is frightened? Old Aldis's room was uninhabitable for days. A ridiculous old pedant.

I didn't know that Laurence Housman was a queer too. (Leo Pavia had the same penchant for romance in a lavatory.) Gow[1] disliked him a good deal, and says he was very tiresome and untrustworthy over A.E.H.'s manuscript poems. A. and L. must have been vinegar and oil. Affable guests at Trinity frequently ruined their chances of a pleasant dinner by congratulating A. on something that in fact was the work

---

[1] A.S.F. Gow, Eton master and later Fellow of Trinity College, Cambridge.

of L. On such occasions A. spoke no word for the rest of the evening. No one ever mistook him for Old King Cole. Where can one find L.H.'s *Echo de Paris*? I have only his *Victoria Regina* plays, many of which are excellent.

My biro did not slip. My saying about your letters and Cicero's was one of those humorous touches whose point is in meiosis, or if you prefer it litotes, the classic example of which is the young lady's remark that Niagara was a pretty sight. Tuppy Headlam was fond of employing it, but it often misses fire in unskilled hands. But as a matter of fact some of Cicero's letters are very well, though letters about contemporary politics are—to me—unfailingly tedious, e.g. many of Horace Walpole's, though one mustn't say so.

Thank you for V. Wedgwood on Herrick. I found—and incorporated—a good sentence of Edward Thomas, viz 'There is no greater proof of the power of style than in the survival of the work of this trivial vicar'. He was a rum 'un sometimes, viz in his bland assurance to God that He will get no harm from his lewder poems. The eighteenth century of course thought that pompous platitudinarians like Akenside (or Lyttelton!) were better poets.

I have met Ketton-Cremer—one of our East Anglian worthies— and liked him. Didn't he write something good about Gray not long ago? And isn't he a member of the Johnson Club, or was he once there as a guest? At the next meeting C. Hollis will be my neighbour, and I expect Roberts will be worth listening to. I have a horrid feeling that the Secretary may suggest that it is time I wrote another paper. I shall resist stoutly, having no real excuse. It is no good pleading old age, as I rather think that only you and Hollis are younger. Do they ever elect a new member, or does the wraith of old Chapman[1] still bar the way like the angel at the gate of Eden? New blood is wanted as much as in English cricket; it may be that both are moribund—which I must tell you I am rather feeling myself after a G.B. meeting of Woodridge School. And I have a touch of lumbago. To-morrow (when I post this) I go to the memorial service to my cousin Stephen who began life in the Navy and ended as a managing director of the Army & Navy Stores, which sounds somehow incongruous. No odder perhaps than General Birdwood who became Master of Peterhouse, or, vice versa

[1] R.W. Chapman, Johnsonian scholar and editor of Jane Austen.

Freyberg who I believe was a dentist. Not that many a dentist does not deserve the V.C.

You did not, I hope, miss the mention of that vicar who wants flogging back in the penal code for young delinquents. His parish, believe it or not, is Much Birch near Hereford. How delighted the boys at Eton were when Jackie Chute, whom they liked (rightly) but thought a bit of an ass (also rightly), became rector of Piddlehinton.

Where is that tremendous epitaph on the grave of a child that died as soon as it was born?

> When th' archangels trump shall blow,
> And souls to bodies join,
> Many will wish their lives below
> Had been as short as mine.

P.S. Love to Ruth.

1 *March 1959*   *Bromsden Farm*

I have often vowed never again to publish any book that I can't read in the original—i.e. in French or English. The people whose opinions one is forced to follow on other languages are often would-be translators in need of work and money, so that one can't wholly trust them. But then I remember that far my biggest seller was a German book—*Seven Years in Tibet*—and then I weaken and let through some horror. (Years ago I published a book on Yugoslavia which had clearly been written by the Godfrey Winn of Sweden—ugh!). The more factual such a book is, the safer: directly one ventures into 'works of art', real or intended, they are apt to suffer a hideous sea-change. All this is by way of preamble to the announcement that I have spent *all* today and yesterday reading the translation of a 750-page German autobiography, for which I have already paid the translator £600.[1] It's rather a good and interesting book, but far, *far* too long, and will clearly have to be so expensive that no-one will buy it—oh dear, it has quite flattened me out. In fact I probably thought it better than it is because I was able to read much of it sitting on the lawn in my shirt-

[1] *The Owl of Minerva* by Gustav Regler (1959).

sleeves. I thought of you in your summer-house and hoped you were sunbound too. All our yellow crocuses have rushed into bloom, and every bird was singing.

Adam's soccer-side must have slacked off last week, for their winning margins were only 6–0, 6–0, and 9–0. They have now scored 90 goals in seven games and are, understandably, top of the League. Apparently the four top sides now play it off in semi-finals and final— it sounds a funny arrangement to me.

I loved your Great Wall of China sayings: did you make them up? The first one reminds me of Yeats's lines:

> Be secret and exult,
> Because of all things known
> This is most difficult.

I quote from memory, since it is late and I have no time to browse happily through W.B.Y. I'll try and find you a copy of *Echo de Paris* on my Berwick Market stall or elsewhere. You emerged triumphant from your Ciceronian comparison, and my umbrage is reduced.

Ketton-Cremer is once again President of the Johnson Club, so you'll see him on March 10. I wish I was going to be with you, but the Lit. Soc. is apt to get into a tangle without its shepherd.

On Tuesday last Ruth and I went to Elisabeth Beerbohm's funeral service at Golders Green. I had stupidly not realised it would be a Jewish service and so had no hat to keep on. We hid behind a pillar, and afterwards Jonah was bragging a bit because of his battered old Homberg. S.C. Roberts (wearing an even older one) gave an excellent address, and so did Dr Garten, the German master at Westminster. Next day I spent the evening with E's sister and brother-in-law near Swiss Cottage. They are German–Jewish refugees: he a lawyer and she a librarian. They gave me Rhine wine, biscuits spread with various excellent condiments, coffee, sweets and a small cigar, and couldn't have been nicer. They're both highly intelligent and may well be easier to deal with than E, since they have no emotional undertones in discussing Max and his works. One day I lunched with the Birkenheads, one with the directors of W.H. Smith, one with thirty-four other men (including Sir William Haley, the Dean of St Paul's, the Swedish Ambassador and Uncle T. Cobbleigh) in the holy of holies at

Lloyd's (grub and company both A.1.). The new Chairman, Tony Grover, was an army friend of mine. I also went to a theatre, to a cocktail party, and dined with Eric Linklater—a week so busy that I staggered down here exhausted on Friday.

Have you yet summoned up courage to tackle *Redgauntlet*? I shall certainly get the new biography of Ethel Smyth, whom I knew slightly in 1930–31—a splendid old creature.

Goodnight, dear George.

5 *March 1959*   *London*

Damn! This will be a miserable letter. Rule 1 in correspondence is—have the letter you are answering before you. Well that is my invariable practice. Your letter duly arrived on Saturday, just as we were about to set off hither. I read it once (i.e. with two more perusals to follow) and then, if you please, left it behind. And, my memory having long gone with the wind, I cannot properly answer it.

I don't like London—too many people and not enough of them nice to look at, or to listen to, and *all* with vile manners as soon as they are at the steering-wheel of a car. Every human being is said to have a soul—but in the tube at the rush hour??

Tell me *exactly* two things. *A Taste of Honey*.[1] Alan Dent condemns it heartily, and half the rest of the critics condemn *him* for doing so. It sounds muck, but what do *you* think? And I see Wilfred Feinburgh's book has been boosted through five editions already.[2] Is it any good, or is my suspicion well-founded that a great number of people buy and read a book *solely* because the Press convinces them that all the Joneses are reading it? Few statements irritate me more than 'this is a book which no one can afford to miss', the unwritten end of which is 'or the Joneses will despise you'. What bilge it all is!

To-morrow I lunch with the Archbishop, the G.B.A. committee being the guests of the Mercers' Company (perhaps 'at the same table

[1] A play of low life in Salford by the nineteen-year-old Shelagh Delaney, recently transferred to the West End from the Theatre Royal. I later saw it in New York and enjoyed it very much.
[2] *No Love For Johnnie*.

as the A.' would more exactly tell the truth, but he is a genial old bird, and at our last meeting accused me afterwards of scowling at him when he was speaking. Archbishop Laud would not have noticed if anyone had scowled at him—or cared), and to-morrow evening my brother has a party. A distinguished civil servant called Sedgwick will be there—a grandson I fancy of the old geologist Adam S. of Cambridge.

Those Chinese sayings are from Geoffrey Madan's collection.[1] I don't *think* he invented them, but wouldn't have put it past him. Next week I will send you another little handful. He had a sharp eye for anything in any way apt, culled from any quarter, e.g. an Underground notice 'Stand on the right and let the rest pass you'—as good as many axioms from the New Testament.

I got a nice dry grin from the Eton Rambler fixtures etc, just arrived. From last year's record two adjacent entries:

	No. of innings	highest score	total	average
R.P. Fleming	1	0	0	0
P.D. Hart-Davis	1	0	0	0

(I won't swear to the last two columns)

My lumbago is on the way out; but I now have a slight pain in the place occupied, I believe, by my liver. I suspect cirrhosis. Watch the paper for bulletins. But Amsler[2] once said in his blunt way 'You're like all perfectly healthy men; your skin itches a little after a midge-bite, and you think you've got leprosy.'

I must stop. Next week I will say all I *meant* to say to-day. I hope the Johnson dinner won't be too dreary. Good old Jonah is coming as a guest.

P.S. My brother told me this advice from a doctor 'Take things more easily,' adding what the doctor did not say—'as the psychiatrist said to a kleptomaniac.'

---

[1] *Livre Sans Nom*, five anonymous pamphlets (1929–1933).
[2] Eton doctor.

I don't think you missed much by leaving my last letter behind: I'm sure there was nothing in it, and you did beautifully without. I bet you aren't in your summer-house today. Here the North Wind howls and I stoke up the library fire: last week-end, as I thought at the time, was a dream.

Idiotically I have only just realised (or remembered) that you were part-editor of *An Eton Poetry Book*. It came out during my last year at Eton, I bought it immediately, learnt most of it by heart and have treasured it ever since. My children have enjoyed it too, and the volume has a comfortably worn look. I don't suppose I had opened it for twenty years until for no conscious reason I took it down yesterday. I had remembered it as solely Alington's work, so your name on the title-page was a lovely surprise, and I'm delighted to find that I think the book just as excellent as I thought it in 1925. There can never have been a better anthology for stirring boys' enthusiasm: the selections first-class, and so well printed and arranged. Thank you, dear George, for the pleasure you gave me long ago and yesterday. Was the book a big seller? It should have been. And is it out of print now? I hope not.

Last week I spent the best part of two days with my German auto-biographer, and despite my general antipathy to Germans I came to like him very much. He has a splendid sense of humour, and his life story is amazing. I persuaded him to cut thousands of words out of the book, which will be a help.

The only way I could answer your question about *A Taste of Honey* would be by going to see the damned thing—from which I recoil. The same goes for the Feinburgh book, which I'm sure is rubbish: surely we get enough about the lower ranks of the Labour Party in the news-papers? Stop worrying about them both: you are in no remotest danger of ossifying mentally. What you say of literary fashion and 'keeping up with the Joneses' is partly true in this country, and wholly so in America. Once when I was there, the two books which were in every-one's drawing-room (mostly unopened) were *The Waves* by Virginia Woolf and a book called *How to Win Friends and Influence People*. It seemed to me inconceivable that *anyone* could enjoy them *both*, and I'm sure they were simply social assets. However, it doesn't much matter if a good book is bought for the wrong reasons. The author has earned royalties, and the chances are that eventually many of the copies will fall into appreciative hands. The great tragedy is when a first-rate book doesn't sell at all, for then there are no copies to fall into anyone's hands. The only thing in favour of 'remaindering' unsold books is that the copies are at least circulating rather than rotting in the publisher's warehouse.

Do send me some more Madaniana. After his death I went laboriously into the question of publishing a book of them, chosen by John Sparrow, but G.M.'s widow proved more intransigent than eight prima donnas, so I retired gracefully.

Peter Green (a very intelligent young man) sent me a proof of his life of Kenneth Grahame, which I am half-way through. K.G. I find both pathetic and distasteful: I'd be amused to know your reaction.

The Obscenity committee met last week, with A.P.H. in great form. I dined one night at the Athenaeum with Wyndham Ketton-Cremer, and lunched another day with Ronald Searle, whom I found as charming as his drawings have always seemed to me revolting—which is to say, exceedingly. (Sorry about that sentence.) He is a great Max fan, and we talked mostly of him.

Peter is now thinking (Ssh! it's a secret, so keep it dark) of writing a book about Younghusband's expedition to Lhasa in 1903–04. I think only one participant (F.M. Bailey) still survives.

And now I must write some notes on a delicious little bombshell of a book about Dickens and his actress-mistress, of which you shall hear more anon.[1] Tomorrow will start off dismally with another funeral at Golders Green—that of the wife of Jonathan Cape's partner, who was also my partner from 1932 to 1940. I only hope I shall be buried in Swaledale with a few villagers following the coffin. Golders Green gives me the creeps—Jewish or otherwise.

[1] *Dickens Incognito* by Felix Aylmer (1959).

35

There was a good gathering to hear Roberts who was entertaining
on 'Estimate' Brown[1] of whom I knew exactly as much as the Corin-
thians knew about the Holy Ghost. We dined in much too small a
room in the Cheshire Cheese after picking our squalid way past spittoons and fag-ends. It is all rather a hugger-mugger affair (especially
compared with the Lit. Soc.). *After* the meal had begun the secretary
tried to make me propose the health of the guests. I stoutly resisted,
and he pushed it onto a pink and portly man, called Butler, unknown
to me, who did it admirably. Jonah was there, guest of Ketton-Cremer,
but I saw very little of him. Another guest was that distinguished
invalid, John Hayward, whom I expect you know. How *did* he get that
really horrifying lip (lower)? One feels that *some*thing could and should
have been done about it. De Beer,[2] Basil Willey,[3] old Uncle L.F.
Powell[4] and all were there, but I seem to be able to *name* fewer of them
every time. The summer meeting is to be at Brighthelmstone, and a
member volunteered to read a paper with suspicious celerity, for are
not those who *want* to read papers rarely among the good ones?

How kind you are about the *Eton Poetry Book*. It is, I think, out of
print now, and never had very much of a sale. Macmillan's didn't do
much about it and always maintained that its title was against it, but
Cyril Alington insisted on it. It is true the relevance of it is not very
clear. My copy always opens at 'Little Orphant Annie' which I tried
to eliminate, but Cyril was mysteriously keen on it. One or two reviews rightly derided it, but mostly such reviews as the book got
were quite cordial. One infuriated me. I did practically all of the stuff
about the poems and poets, and some ass regretted that readers should
be 'told what to think about them'. As no doubt you (and everyone
else with eyes) saw, the main gist was to record what *had* been thought
or said about them, very often inviting readers to differ, e.g Coleridge
(was it?) saying that Blanco White's sonnet was 'the finest and most

[1] John Brown, Scottish clergyman and poet (1715–1766) published *An
Estimate of the Manners and Principles of the Times* in 1757.

[2] Esmond de Beer (b. 1895), editor of Evelyn's Diary and Locke's
Correspondence.

[3] Professor of English Literature at Cambridge and author (1897–1979).

[4] Johnsonian scholar and editor (1881–1975).

grandly conceived'—I think I quote right—'in the language'.[1] Surely *very* high among rules for critics is 'Never use superlatives'.

I will send you some more of Madan next week. His widow shilly-shallied endlessly about his book, of which several copies were distributed among his friends. I didn't get one, and wasn't of the inner circle. A remark of mine, however, *is* in the book—ascribed to Gaillard Lapsley, that admirable U.S.A. Trinity don who invariably embarrassed one with his ultra-perfect manners. You remember Michael Finsbury, who dressed too much like a wedding-guest to be quite a gentleman.[2]

I had a pleasant little chat with the Archbishop last week. He was most genial; in fact if you described us as 'buddies,' nobody could cavil. The Mercers' Hall where we lunched was rebuilt last year and must have cost an astronomical sum—so vast that the Insurance policy on it forbids any smoking. And at the general meeting after a lunch at which Lucullus would have opened his eyes (and, of course, his mouth) I always look forward to 'abstract my mind and think of Tom Thumb'[3] and enjoying a Monte Cristo cigar out of my opulent son-in-law's Xmas box. But I enjoyed the masterly chairmanship of the Archbishop. They tell me he can be very ratty if opposed, but I have never seen it.

I hope you told Virginia Woolf about *The Waves* being on the same table as *How to Win Friends etc.* Would she have laughed or not? You never can tell with the *genus irritabile.* (What, by the way, has happened to Leonard Merrick and his books—invariably praised by the critics and quite or nearly unread by the public? I cannot recollect ever reading one.)

Tell me all about the Lit. Soc. (including the food of course). It is much better fun—and cheaper!—than the Johnson dinner, and one rarely sees a spittoon, or hears one being used.

[1] Joseph Blanco White (1775–1841), an Irish–Spanish theological writer, composed one sonnet in 1825 called 'Night and Death', the only thing he is remembered for.

[2] In Stevenson's *The Wrong Box*, chapter 8.

[3] 'When Charles Fox said something to me once about Catiline's Conspiracy, I withdrew my attention and thought about Tom Thumb.' (Doctor Johnson)

Kenneth Grahame. I shall read his life. A pitiable man apparently, but who can say those three books are anything but delicious, one would say the work of a serene and delightful man. I always liked *The Golden Age* and *Dream Days* better than *The Wind in the Willows*. As for e.g. 'The Reluctant Dragon' tale—but what did I say about superlatives? But dash it all, what else can one use about, say, the talk between St George and the Dragon before the fight—St G. indicating a spot on the vast body which he could safely prod with his spear, and the dragon demurring, as it was a ticklish place and it would never do if he laughed during the battle. I look forward to reading the Dickens book. The scabrous and salacious old Agate used to aver that D. 'tumbled' half the women he met and all the housemaids—but it may have been wishful thinking.

Of course you must be buried in Swaledale—but not yet, please.

Did I ever read you my poem in which Golders Green was mentioned? My only poem in print!

15 March 1959   *36 Soho Square*

Sunday is much the pleasantest—or least disagreeable—day in London: little noise or traffic and fewer of those hideous people that so displease you. I got back from Cambridge at lunch-time and went to the nearest Lyons (usually jostling with people), where I consumed a (believe it or not) Wimpey Cheeseburger, some coffee and a strawberry ice. The W.C. was composed of a hot bun containing a hamburger, onion and cheese—much better than it sounds. Here (No 36) I found your letter, which had just missed me on Friday, when I caught the 4.30 train from Liverpool Street. Geoffrey Keynes met me at Cambridge and drove me out to his house at Brinkley (about thirteen miles). It's a pleasant Jane Austenish house with three acres of garden. They (G. and Mrs G., who was a Darwin, sister of Sir Charles and of Gwen Raverat, cousin of Bernard, grand-daughter of *The Origin of Species*) gave me a huge dinner, after which we sat in G's incredible library and he showed me rarity after rarity: goodness knows what his books are worth. I got to bed exhausted at midnight. On Saturday morning G. drove me back to Cambridge, where I lunched in Trinity

Hall with Graham Storey, who is editing the Dickens letters for me. Oh yes—before that Geoffrey took me for a walk by the Backs, over King's Bridge where the crocuses carpeted the ground in full bloom. We penetrated the dim religious light of King's Chapel, and G. thoroughly enjoyed showing me everything. Did you know that Maynard Keynes, by wise speculation, doubled King's income and then left them all his books and pictures as well as half a million in cash? Geoffrey had to sign a cheque for £243,000 in favour of the Revenue for death duties!

In the afternoon Storey drove me to Madeline House's, where I talked for an hour before taking a taxi back to the Provost's Lodge at King's. My fellow-guests were Lord Bridges (charming and very young for his age) and a couple called Wollheim (he a philosophy don at London University). I slept in Noel's study (very comfortable) and while we were changing for dinner all the lights fused. Nothing daunted, we joined another 150 chaps and consumed the enclosed delectable dinner. I sat on the Provost's right(!!). On my other side was Maurice Hill, a delightful geo-physicist and nephew of Geoffrey Keynes. Afterwards the whole gathering adjourned to the Lodge, where I managed to sober up on four tumblers of orangeade. I talked to many, known and unknown, among them Leslie Hotson, Dadie Rylands, E.M. Forster (rather deaf now in a crowd but otherwise un-aged) and a young don called Michael Jaffé, who insisted that when he was an undergraduate (some ten years ago) I had given one of the only three tolerable talks to some literary society in Cambridge. Even if he was confusing me with someone else (as I assured him) this was agreeably gratifying. I got to bed by 1 a.m., and was brought my breakfast in bed, with the *Observer*, at 9. And so back to London. I had a long talk with Noel about Adam's future, and am more than ever inclined to think he should go to Cambridge (i.e. King's) rather than Oxford. Noel says they are most anxious to get more scientists from Eton, and he (Adam) should be able to get some sort of scholarship or grant. What do you think?

John Hayward has some sort of progressive muscular atrophy, about which nothing can be done: he's certainly not a pretty sight, poor chap. I read some Leonard Merrick years ago, and thought him NO GOOD: perhaps that's why he never sold.

Please produce your poem on Golders Green as soon as possible. And pray for me on Wednesday evening, when in a hostelry called the Nag's Head I have to address the assembled Book-Collectors of Manchester. Afterwards I stay the night with Phoebe Hesketh near Bolton. WHAT can I say to the brutes? I can't use the Emperor Gordian every time—oh dear![1]

19 March 1959 *Grundisburgh*

Of course it was bound to come, and I am back again in the armchair and inflicting upon you—now what would Henry James have called the Biro? (It would have been a good question for my Extra Studies in old days. I wish I had kept the five 'Little Jack Horners' rewritten in the style of Pope which led the chairman of Cammell Laird —a civilised business-man, financier etc—to say, after reading twenty specimens, that if any of these five wanted a start in C.L. they should have it). Of course you remember H.J.'s apologies for his typewriter— never called a typewriter but such things as 'this graceless mechanism', 'this bleak legibility' etc. The thermometer is on the wrong side of 40°, and hare or venison could be preserved for days in the summer house without any danger of approaching that height of ripeness which Dr Johnson would have found superlatively toothsome.

I am disgusted at your not getting my last letter by the first post on Friday. It was posted in *London* on Thursday afternoon, in Northumberland Avenue, just outside the Royal Empire Society (but on the very next day there was a man chiselling away changing Empire to Commonwealth. Deplorable! 'Empire' and 'Imperial' are fine words, Commonwealth isn't). I suppose postmen are as slack about 'service' as other nationalised workers. They used not to be.

I read in yesterday's *Times* that there is quite likely to be a printers'

---

[1] 'Twenty-two acknowledged concubines and a library of 62,000 volumes attested the variety of his inclinations, and from the productions which he left behind him it appears that the former as well as the latter were designed for use rather than for ostentation.' (Gibbon on the Emperor Gordian)

strike. Do you know about that; and how does it hit publishers? The last one was just before our correspondence began. How hateful these strikes are. I don't believe e.g. German workers have this brutal indifference to national interests. And I see some genial chap wants the Burnham scale to plump for a 20% increase in teachers' salaries next October. That would mean goodbye to many independent schools.

Your last letter gave me an odd turn, for the first line I happened to read was 'The W.C. was composed of a hot bun'. This, I thought, must be *Alice in Wonderland* brought up to date. No novel or story in 1959 but must mention the W.C., and made of a bun is just what it might have been in the White Rabbit's house. I have never heard of a Wimpey Cheeseburger. I shall look out for it. And strawberry ice! Your time at Cambridge sounds pleasant. The Backs perhaps you saw about a month too early. I remember days when no comment was possible beyond 'By Gum!' Maynard Keynes, I always heard, so manipulated the King's money that from having been about the poorest college, financially, he made it the richest. And the queer thing is that his first essays in speculation were completely unsuccessful. Did you know him? Very courteous and kind, and with a mind of frankly terrifying swiftness in ordinary talk. What talk I had with him, you will be surprised to hear, was never about finance. His death, like Temple's, was infuriatingly untimely. Did King's Chapel impress you? Surely yes. Gow told me that Lovell of Queen's, Oxford, some sort of expert on buildings, and clearly looking at architecture as Leavis looks at literature, on entering King's Chapel, looked at the roof and murmured 'Bestial'.

I was talking to the Leys School intelligentsia on Monday and, *inter alia*, derided the Leavis view—not mentioning his name. I must tell Ivor Brown that nothing delighted them more than his version of the Lord's prayer rendered into a blend of civil service and commercial English. 'That our daily intake of cereal filler be not in short supply' is nauseatingly good.

Roger enjoyed his Lit. Soc. dinner between as he put it 'Fergusson (merry) and Sargent (polished).' Your fare was better than the Cheshire Cheese bully beef. Your King's menu is mouth-watering too —the hand of Keynes is visible in the left-hand [wine] column. Oscar

Browning and Walter Headlam had to put up with the sort of beverage that Uncle Pentstemon ('uttering a kind of large hiccup') derided as 'grocer's stuff'.[1] H.G.W. describing a plebeian wedding-breakfast was flawless in humour and perception.

You are right about Lord Bridges. Is Wollheim the author of a belittling view of Walter Bagehot, whom everyone else praises very highly, and did you like him? His review of the book gave the impression that he would be surprised to find Wollheim wrong in any way. G.M. Young puts B. at the very top of the Victorians. Michael Jaffé is an amiable fellow, some say a little too anxious to please. But what harm in that, when so many are the reverse? Dadie Rylands, I hope, is well and happy, but why is he not writing anything these days? Up to the neck in dramatics I suspect. He was a grand audience in A and B extra studies and is particularly pleasant to meet. It is a pity he can't or won't write letters. Arthur Benson made the same complaint when D.R. was an undergraduate. E.M. Forster I never knew. I wish I had.

Surely you would do well to send Adam to King's. I hear very well of it nowadays under its youthful Provost. I don't believe you could do better, though of course my knowledge of Oxford is scanty.

Another handful of Chinese sayings:

The Three Rare Things
(Sights of the Kingfisher)

1) Clear memory of Romantic conversation.
2) The meeting of Great Equals.
3) Unremarked abbreviation of Pious Exercises.★

★(This beats me, but it has a mysterious charm)

The Three Foolish Things
(Spring Lambs)

1) Deep sleep in an Unknown House.
2) Setting to sea in a Borrowed Junk.
3) Not to lag behind when the Elephant approaches a New Bridge.

---

[1] In *The History of Mr Polly* by H.G. Wells.

Are you *sure* I haven't sent you my one printed poem—to Plum Warner? I told it to Ivor Brown who smiled—not unkindly—and then gave full and accurate information to Tommy Lascelles and me about Golder.

P.S. I am deep in *Redgauntlet*. Very good but I do sometimes murmur 'Get *on*, get *on*, old dear.'

22 *March 1959*   *Bromsden Farm*

So far, thank goodness, I know nothing of a printers' strike, but anything that would slow down the flood of unnecessary books and give me a few free days for Oscar would be most welcome. I loved the new lot of 'Chinese sayings'. You certainly haven't ever sent me your poem, so please do. You sound rather half-hearted about my beloved *Redgauntlet*: I must read it again myself—but when?

Last week was somewhat interrupted by my journeying on Wednesday to Manchester to be the guest of honour at the annual dinner of the Manchester Society of Book-Collectors. I had relied on the four-hour train-journey to compose my speech, but a resolutely affable chemical engineer from Macclesfield insisted on talking most of the way, and I arrived with only a few notes scribbled on a small piece of paper. It was very hot in the upper room at the Old Nag's Head and I had *two* stout table-legs where my knees should have been. I was between the President, an H.M.I. who recently published a bibliography of Chesterton, and his wife, who won my heart by immediately saying she hated Manchester and hankered for her home in the south. The dinner was plain but adequate, my speech neither, but once again I got away with the Emperor Gordian—God bless you! Then *four* people made speeches saying what a splendid chap I was, and the party broke up into general conversation. They were all very friendly and appreciative and I was glad I'd gone. Then Phoebe Hesketh drove me to her home near Bolton, and next morning we walked on the moors and flushed three curlew (or curlews?) before I caught the London train at Wigan. On it I had the best train-lunch I've ever had in this country—but that was nothing to the superb dinner I consumed that evening (menu enclosed). It may not read interestingly, but every drop and morsel were quite first-class. It was the dinner given by my father's stockbroking firm to celebrate his retirement after sixty years. Everybody, I think, had been dreading it for weeks, but (as so often in meetings with my father) your cousin Oliver saved the day with his eupeptic humour and made the whole thing a great success. I told him my father had got his doctor to give him some sort of stimulant to get him through the evening, and as soon as Oliver saw the old boy he said: 'Hullo, Richard, I hear they've given you a subcutaneous injection of Bollinger 49'—which delighted the old fellow. I sat between Anthony (Lyttelton, of course) and my cousin Ian Cameron, well away from my father's business contemporaries, several of whom (particularly Alfred Wagg) looked as though they'd been exhumed for the evening. But they were all charming, and the whole occasion was rather touching. Goodness knows what the old boy will do with his time now. For years I suspect that he has been nothing but a nuisance in the office, but the effort of getting there and back occupied most of his day.

Adam reports that his boys'-maid has got her own television set, and he wonders whether the Welfare State hasn't gone a little too far. His side is now in the final of the Junior Soccer League. Their semi-final score of 4–0 was rather a come-down.

On Thursday, as perhaps I told you, Ruth is flying to Italy to spend a fortnight with her daughter. My horror of aeroplanes greatly adds to my reluctance to be without her so long, and she's not tremendously keen on it herself. The post to and from Italy is incredibly bad. Oh well, I shall try to catch up with my work while she's away.

I invested a small sum on Oscar Wilde in the National, but he fell at the fourth fence.

25 March 1959   *Grundisburgh*

Odd! Whenever I get a letter from you in which you say you are practically down and out, smothered with work and fatigue, I know that it is going to be a particularly good one. Rather like Brahms, who wrote to someone that he had 'had to insert' into his violin concerto 'a feeble slow movement'—and proceeded to charm everybody (except E.M. Forster) with the most delicious thing in the world. And Kipling's 'Recessional' was retrieved from the waste-paper basket wherein he had chucked it as not up to much.

No, I did enjoy *Redgauntlet*, but now and then got impatient with the conversation, almost every item of which resembled a passage to be put into Latin Prose. I know I should be made of sterner stuff. You clearly had a great success at Manchester. I have long adopted the plan of pleading deafness to a garrulous fellow-traveller, in fact I have always disliked talking in the train to anyone—sometimes breaking my rule when there are only two of us in the carriage. What *did* you have to say to the chemical engineer? Was your talk of hydrogen and litmus paper? I am glad the Emperor Gordian came in useful again. My brother who is always speechifying to audiences interested in iron and steel, and extolling the advantages of co-operation, also has a winner (I think I found it in some digest in a dentist's waiting-room). An advertisement: 'Communist with own knife and fork would like to meet Communist with own steak-and-kidney pie.' And he often uses Walter Hagen's remark on the *first* tee of the *first* round of the open championship 'Well, boys, who's going to be second?' And then did actually proceed to win it. Positively Miltonic!

Curlew I am sure is right as against curlews. I always liked Mr Squeers's saying 'twenty pound', and in fact, as often as not, my father did. Is that singular used now for anything but fish? 'Trouts' would ensure blackballing at any club. Shall I try it at the Lit. Soc?

I send you the menu of C.M. Wells's birthday dinner (*aetat* eighty-eight, and he looks about fifty-six). The Burgundy he took two sips of and said 'A little disappointing. It is good but I expected it to be superb.' John Christie[1] was there. He has let his white hair grow and now has a strong resemblance to Thackeray, with a hint of Luxmoore, with neither of whom he has an iota in common. Plum Warner wasn't there, on, I fear, the slightly risible grounds that after dark he is afraid of being either run over or coshed. And yet half-a-century ago he stood up to Ernest Jones like a man—the man even W.G. admitted was 'fast', which adjective he wouldn't wholly allow to Richardson,

---

[1] Eccentric millionaire (1882–1962). For some years a master at Eton. Founded the Glyndebourne Music Festival on his own estate 1934.

if you please. C.B. Fry said Jones was too quick to hook even when he pitched half way. Wells in 1901 had Woodcock on his MCC side v Eton. I made 22 against him—nearly all through the slips. I played at his first delivery as it plopped into the wicket-keeper's hands. Wells reminded me that as his side came onto the field, Woodcock, knowing that schoolboys had never seen anyone nearly as fast, said to him, 'Shall I slip 'em down, sir?' and got the reply 'What do you mean? Bowl your ordinary stuff.'

I hope old Alfred Wagg is well. He left Benson's before I arrived, and I met him only half a dozen times, but what a kind and friendly fellow he always was. I suppose he was at Eton with your father.

You are not, I presume, listening to some rather dreary reminiscences of Galsworthy, who does not sound a very lively companion— so buttoned-up, and serious and habit-ridden. Still he created old Heythorp—who would have derided him vigorously! Match me that marvel. How the young moderns despise him, and how little they ultimately matter. I read that Malcolm Muggeridge likens Macmillan in Russia to a character out of the Forsyte Saga, by which, no doubt, he means the lowest depth of outmoded futility (would Galsworthy have been amused by the lady who said she had recently seen a comedy— Gallstones by Milesworthy? I am afraid not).

I am pretty sure my Xmas letter to Percy Lubbock at Lerici never reached him. He hasn't answered, but I fear he is in a poorish way— quite blind now, and immensely fat, and sad, a good deal, apparently, sponged on by various young men. And villas are springing up all round Gli Scafari, though as to that blindness must be a boon.

I enclose my doggerel. Few people realise how easy that sort of stuff is to write. One idea and a handful of words that rhyme is all that is wanted. And the result imposes on dear simpletons like P.F.W. who actually wrote 'What a brain is yours!'

P.S. I agree with you (and Winston) about aeroplanes, and try to reassure myself by remembering the milkman's reply to a complaint that one day his milk was sour. 'Think, lady, on how many days it *isn't* sour.'

To P.F.W. on his birthday, shortly after the practice had started of naming streets, courts etc after well-known Londoners.

Why some names entirely perish
Like stones in the depth of the sea,
While others we honour and cherish,
Has always caused wonder to me.
For instance, does anyone hold a-
-n idea (I've forgotten it clean)
Of who in the wide world was Golder
Who made that unpopular Green?
Opinion grows daily that Potter
Whose Bar's in the county of Herts,
Was in truth a good deal of a rotter,
Of wholly contemptible parts.
But I think that one might have been fonder
Of him—though not quite as a friend—
Than that lumpish nonentity Ponder,
Who is known far and wide for his End.
Far and wide? I can see you are grinning
And think my veracity's small,
For of Ponder, his end or beginning,
We frankly know nothing at all.
And so with them all; it is really
An incontrovertible fact
That of none is known, dimly or clearly,
A single word, thought, look, or act.
Oblivion scatters her poppy,
But for reasons quite obvious to all
They've resolved this old custom to copy,
And glorify street, court and hall
Throughout London—the names that adorn her
Strike a note that will never be dumb,
For among them rings out that of Warner
Known—and loved—the world over as Plum.

Easter Day, 29 March 1959   *Bromsden Farm*

These four days have come as a blessed respite, and today it has
been too wet for anything but the library fire. Each night I catch up

47

hours of lost sleep, and am generally so relaxed that I am almost coma-tose. I've even brought down my Oscar Wilde footnotes, so that I can remember what they're all about, and maybe take up the task in London next week. We have no children here, so peace reigns. Adam's team won the Soccer final 5–0, and their total score for eleven games is 118–0. He says the cup is the second smallest in the school, the smallest being the Junior Chess Cup, which he won last half.

I loved your poem, and don't wonder old Plum was pleased. Many thanks for the excellent Communist-with-own-knife-and-fork joke, which I shall salt away to astonish some other collection of credulous provincials.

My darling Ruth flew off to Milan on Thursday, and will be away for a fortnight. The light grows dim while she's away, but I shall use the time to try and get all my publishing work up to date. She has been taken to Florence for Easter, and just as I was imagining her sightseeing in brilliant sunshine, I heard on the radio that in Rome the Pope gave his blessing in pouring rain. Contrariwise, my sister reports on the telephone from Argyllshire that they've had a lovely sunny day. Thank God we weren't marching from Aldermaston!

The C.M.W. menu is almost Galsworthian in its superb simplicity, and I like the club's having printed even the date in French. I only hope I shall be enjoying Burgundy at eighty-eight. My father at eighty confines himself to whisky and kümmel in very large and frequent doses.

I have been finishing *Heroes and Hero-Worship*, begun many months ago, and have specially enjoyed all the stuff about Cromwell in the last chapter. I think it will have to be *The French Revolution* next.

I expect you saw that our Obscenity Bill got surprisingly well through its Standing Committee. Next week the Herbert Committee meets to discuss tactics for the last lap—Report and Third Reading (the Lords are considered a pushover, if you'll forgive the phrase).

I'm also enjoying the new biography of Ethel Smyth.[1] Her friend the Empress Eugénie invariably referred to the Franco-Prussian War and the overthrow of the Second Empire simply as '*les événements*', which is almost Dickensian in its charm.

---

[1] By Christopher St John (1959).

Next Friday is said to be Neville Cardus's seventieth birthday (though in his autobiography I'm pretty sure he says he was born in 1890) and a big luncheon is to be given him in the restaurant of the Festival Hall. I have subscribed and shall go.

Monday morning

The sun is shining, but black clouds loom. I have been lingering deliciously over my coffee, toast and marmalade, unable to put down *The French Revolution*. What a magnificent opening, with every stop pulled out and sounding. I care not whether the history is exact and rejoice in the book as literature—surely the greatest piece of sustained rhetoric in the language. When did you last read it? I can't wait to go on, but the garden is calling, and I am in the middle of relaying a brick path—a soothing therapeutic task which I enjoy. Occasionally Fleming rides by on a foaming horse, otherwise nothing intrudes on the rustic solitude. And mercifully I have a great ability to dismiss from my mind the worries of tomorrow—the hideous pile of letters on my office desk, no Ruth to guide me, the telephone, the printers' delays and all the rest of it. I imagine you in your summer-house, perhaps with some of your countless descendants sporting round you. I heard Humphrey's band on the radio the other day, but alas it is not my cup of tea. The problem of the generations is too great. But there are plenty of other things to enjoy, if only one had the time.

1 April 1959   *Grundisburgh*

'Comatose'! Nirvana—that is the right holiday aim. It is all piling up nutriment, like the camel's hump—or is that a legend from Pliny or Herodotus, or the Rev. Wood[1], one of whom records that the lion's hatred for the hyena is such that if their skins are hung near each other, 'the lion's skin will immediately fall away'? Anyway I hope you are now entirely rested and dealing with that ghastly pile that confronted you yesterday (Host pressing eminent lawyer to have another drink and at last lawyer: 'Well thank you, yes; I shall find a huge pile

[1] The Rev. John George Wood (1827–1889), voluminous writer of popular natural history.

49

of letters to answer when I get home.' Host: 'But how will another drink help you to answer them?' L. 'It won't—but it will help to create that state of mind in which I don't care whether they are answered or not.').

I knew you would appreciate the C.M.W. menu. He always had three gastronomic *bêtes noires*, i.e. sherry or cocktail, soup, and sweet. I agree with him to a great extent—though I have come across some very affable soups in my day. And at lunch, of course, a currant-and-raspberry tart, a blackberry fool, a jam omelette, a treacle-pudding—well dash it all. Before we go a step further, I must know whether you are with me so far. There are others too. Which would *you* choose for your last lunch before execution?

I am delighted by your liking for Carlyle. He has always been a favourite of mine, though I have latterly kept quiet about him; so many find him rebarbative and don't recognise power when they meet it ('*Une des plus grandes preuves de médiocrité, c'est de ne pas savoir reconnaître la supériorité là où elle se trouve*'—another of Geoffrey Madan's, written apparently by one J.B. Say, whoever he may have been).[1] Scene after scene in *The F.R.* will—literally—raise your pulse and your rate of breathing. Quite wrong of course for any prose to do so, according to Maugham and Murry *et les autres*. I have been reading lately in bed a good deal of G.M. Young (given, I need hardly say, by R.H-D) and thought repeatedly how wise and perceptive he is. He never lets one down with a shallow or petulant prejudice. What confidence a man gives you who is always out to see the good in writers and men generally, and does very little indeed of that eternal and tedious hole-picking.

Give my regards to Neville Cardus if you have speech with him. I had a good crack with him once, and we began a little correspondence, but it soon became clear he didn't want to keep it up and it lapsed. Someone warned me that he takes up new friends and drops them with equal speed, which may well be, without damning him overmuch. Anyway, a man who wrote those cricket-books—the early ones especially—is sure at least of *my* lasting goodwill.

I envy your Gladstonian power of detachment. I imagine most or all of our great men have had it—Wellington, Churchill etc. Arthur

---

[1] Jean Baptiste Say (1767–1832), French political economist.

Benson once asked old Gladstone if he didn't often lie awake and wonder whether some great decision he had just made was right or not, and got the astonished answer (in broad Lancashire) 'No! Where would be the use of thaat?' I always cherish the memory of Winston in 1940, handed a bankrupt situation by Neville Chamberlain and going off to bed, where he slept eight good hours. Whereas I lie awake half the night if a pipe freezes. And there are fussier folk than I, e.g. the elderly spinster who slept no wink till (at 4 a.m.) she decided on the name for the new kitten—i.e. 'Kitty'. Or if you think that is spurious, I can beat it with almost any example from the spinstery of Grundisburgh.

I read this morning of a bridge-game at some swell club yesterday where each player held a complete suit—the odds against which are about a quadrillion to one. Pity it happened on April 1, if they really want to be believed.

I share your taste in the matter of Humphrey's music; but all our values are hurrying down the drain. I went to *The Reluctant Debutante* yesterday. They tell me the play was better than the film; the film seemed to me sheer drivel with some smartish backchat, most of which I did not quite catch. But does London really flock to a play in which the point is that a dance-band drummer is a Spanish prince incognito? And Humphrey points out that the difficulty nowadays would be to find a drummer who was a drummer and not a royalty.

I sympathise about Ruth's absence. To point out what fun it will be when she returns is the lunatic's reason for beating his head against the wall—so nice when I stop. But that is all the consolation I can give you—beyond of course the old couplet from Stephen Hawes about the longe day.[1]

5 *April 1959*   *Bromsden Farm*

At last I have seen a real live nuthatch! After tea today it came several times to the bird-table and ate greedily. A neat and pretty little bird, the shape of a kingfisher, with a long beak, a pink chest,

---

[1] For though the daye be never so longe,
   At last the bells ringeth to evensonge.

and a black back as sleek as a seal's. I think the blue-tits disapprove, for one of them did a turn of sentry-go on the table for some time afterwards.

Adam arrived covered with glory. This was his first half as a specialist, and he got a Distinction in Trials, and also the Trials Prize (top of the B Science specialists). This being his third Distinction, he got an extra pound for that! He's not sixteen till July. I opened one of our three bottles of champagne to celebrate his achievements, and all ranks lapped it gratefully up. Duff has mown all the grass, and the croquet season opened to-day. Daffodils are pouring out all round. I expect you've been in your summer-house.

I entirely agree with you (and disagree with C.M.W.) about sweets, and also soups. I can't decide what sweet I'd choose for my last meal—probably apple tart in the end, though I'm very partial to rich concoctions of chestnut purée.

My liking for *The French Revolution* continues, though I haven't got a great deal further, since I purposely left it here, so as to concentrate on other things in London. I have a delightful second edition in three volumes (1839), with an attractive small page: all the one-volume editions are in such tiny print. So you've been re-reading G.M. Young. Poor old boy, it isn't whisky but melancholia that has got him down. He has to have a male nurse in All Souls, and I think Sparrow and the other birds would be much relieved if they could ship the old polymath off to a nursing home—or even to Paradise—for he is a great nuisance to them.

I've always noticed that when cinema-avoiders *do* go to a film, they always choose a rotten one. I could have told you to avoid *The Reluctant Debutante* at all costs. I managed to sit through the play (because Celia Johnson was in it) but that was enough. Also Rex Harrison is just about my least favourite actor. Next time you must ask my advice.

Last week in London was a short one after the holiday, but Ruth's absence made it seem long and empty. (She returns, thank heaven, next Friday. I rang her up in Milan and she's all right, if a trifle homesick.) I went to one unremarkable dinner-party, but mostly worked in the flat. On Friday I attended Cardus's seventieth birthday lunch. It was held in the deserted restaurant of the Festival Hall, and, though those facing the huge windows had a lovely wide view of the river (did you know that the clock on top of the Shell building is known as Big Benzine?) the others (of whom I was one) might have been in any provincial hotel out of season. Forty-seven people turned up, and during the preliminary drinks I had some talk with Ivor Brown (nice as ever but even more liberally spread with scurf, cigarette-ash and shaving-soap than usual), Lady Violet Bonham-Carter (who I think must have strayed in from some other function, since she clearly had no connection with this one), John Arlott and others. The only other cricketer present was John Woodcock, the Cricket Correspondent of *The Times*, but just as I was about to question him about Australia, we were summoned to lunch. I was between an immensely vivacious lady pianist and the No 2. music critic of the *Daily Telegraph*, a pleasant-spoken young man with an Old Wykhamist tie and eyes almost touch-ing (each other, not the tie). Most of the other guests were musicians or critics, with Arthur Bliss and Moiseiwitsch at the top table. It was rather fun, and surprisingly easy, fitting the odd faces to the still odder names which I have so long passed quickly by in newspapers. The genial little foreigner with black hairs growing on the top of his nose could only be Mosco Carner, and naturally the tall bearded Levantine was Felix Aprahamian of the *Sunday Times*, the balding intellectual Desmond Shawe-Taylor, and so on. Malcolm Sargent made a suitable speech and Neville responded. Then some tributes from absent friends were read out—from Ernest Newman, Bruno Walter, etc, and that was that. I think Neville was delighted with it all. He looks just the same as he did twenty-five years ago. The lunch itself was eatable rather than memorable.

Tonight I must review five thrillers, and read (much of it for the third time, and it doesn't grow on me) the latest manuscript of three quarters of the first volume of Stephen Potter's autobiography. Before condemning the vanity of authors (as I do every day) one should re-flect that it is pretty well all they have to sustain them in their lonely task, and that it is present in the great no less than in the minor scribes.

On May 9 I have agreed to take part in another W.H. Smith 'brains trust'—chiefly because it's at Giggleswick School, which I'd love to see. Wasn't Agate there, or do I dream? Anyhow it's in *Yorkshire*, whither, two months today, I shall be blissfully hurrying. You've no idea how, all through the year, Ruth and I dream and scheme in preparation for this brief respite. But then I suppose most people have no such solace.

Cold apple-tart I hope, and then I am with you. George Wyndham practically sacked his cook if she ever sent it up hot. But the practical Pamela says that it is very rare to find cold pastry that is not heavy on the tummy, and she may be right. My view is that of the late Mr Justice Day[1]: 'My stomach has got to take what I give it.'

Please give Adam warm congratulations from me. You must be immensely proud of him. And how nice to think that with such a father he will never be one of those philistine scientists. I like the picture of the H-D family quaffing champagne over an intellectual triumph. Usually the magnum is brought out to celebrate a spillikins victory or such-like (what a solemn fuss they make now about table-tennis, and I see a young lady has marched out on finding that her 'sandwich' racquet was forbidden. Is that the racquet with a thin rubber sheet between two of cork? And why forbidden?).

• You will have passed by now the lovely 'O evening sun of July' in *The French Revolution,* but you have some tremendous things to come. FitzGerald, whose favourite poet was Crabbe, and clearly found it uncomfortable to be roused, wrote in a letter of 'Carlyle's canvas waves', but surely the authentic sea is audible in the great passages. F. had a good deal of the old woman about him (not perhaps in *l'affaire* Posh[2]!) —easily shocked, e.g. by Hardy, George Eliot, and even Browning; and I gather the real Omar had a fine oriental salacity in many lines, expurgated by F. Did you see that long thing on *The Rubaiyat* in the *T.L.S.* in which the writer thanked heaven the Omar Khayyam Club had ceased to exist? But it met last fortnight and does so annually and flourishingly, as a correspondent last week pointed out. Surely the editor should have put a brief apology? I dined there once as a guest,

[1] Sir John Charles Frederic Sigismund Day (1826–1908), Judge in the Queen's Bench Division.

[2] Nickname of Joseph Fletcher, a Lowestoft fisherman to whom FitzGerald was much attached.

but the speeches were disappointing. Oscar Wilde's son was in the chair, and a voluble but unaware American guest made some observations about homosexuality. How cautious one has to be! Do you remember poor old Thackeray facetiously telling a man who had just made a balloon ascent that he couldn't imagine how anyone could do such a thing unless perhaps he was a dentist in ordinary life—and of course it turned out that the man *was*!

I *am* sorry about G.M. Young because I find his stuff immensely repaying. His mere learning is surely quite staggering; and he sometimes makes the characteristic All Souls error of over-rating his readers' knowledge and being teasingly allusive. But he has given me much enjoyment. Now for the Kenneth Grahame book, preparatory to which I have read *The Wind in the Willows*. There is *some* fun in it but much less than in e.g. 'The Reluctant Dragon'. I have a suspicion I shall resent young Peter Green, but maybe not: I look forward to hearing from you and Ruth at *6 p.m. next Tuesday* exactly what I ought to think. Will old Bernard Darwin by any chance be at the Lit. Soc? I should like another crack with him, though he writes better than he talks.

I am glad the Cardus lunch went well, though surely the cricket-world was poorly represented. Is my feeling correct that he is not altogether *persona grata* there? I could not help sending a word of good wishes to N.C., as one who loves his charm and skill with words (perhaps that was why Lady Violet was there?) and have spent an hour this morning re-discovering how unfadingly good *Good Days* and *A Cricketer's Book* are. I once tried to get N.C. made a member of the M.C.C. as the laureate of the game, but failed dismally.

Yes, old Agate was at Giggleswick. Tuppy always alleged that he knew a man called Wigglesworth who lived at Biggleswade and was educated at Giggleswick. But I don't think we believed him. I fancy the clientèle is mainly local.

11 *April 1959*   *Bromsden Farm*

I'm going to try and post this tomorrow, so as to make sure of your getting it before you leave for London. In fact you're lucky to get a letter at all, for on Wednesday morning I woke up with an incipient stye in my eye. It got steadily larger and more crippling, and on Thursday evening I sought out a doctor who gave me three kinds of penicillin (capsules, drops and ointment), which are just now beginning to take effect. As luck would have it, Wednesday and Thursday were two frantically busy days, so that by yesterday I was half-blind and wholly idiotic. Today I have solaced myself by watching the bird-table, where a *pair* of nuthatches have been regular visitors, among tits, chaffinches and robins. And *then*, to delight me, there arrived a spotted woodpecker—black-and-white with a pillar-box-red underside to its tail. Much too big for the table, and immensely shy, constantly climbing up the stem and taking fright before it reached the top.

I'm happy to say my beloved Ruth got home safely last night, though I shan't see her till Monday. I told her my stye was psychosomatic and symbolised my tears at her absence.

On Tuesday, at the bibliographical dining club, I had some talk with Robert Birley and he convinced me that today *Oxford* is in fact the place to send a budding scientist, so, with a sigh of relief and a brief pang for the lost delights of King's, I switch my thoughts back where they belong. Birley was entirely human, forthcoming and *un*-shy, and I enjoyed seeing him. At dinner I sat him between Sparrow and John Hayward.

G.M. Young's assumption of knowledge in his reader I find almost as flattering as irritating. Sometimes I tried to make him explain an allusion for the benefit of the weaker vessels, but he invariably refused incredulously. Nowadays when most writing is directed at the semi-literate I respond to some sort of a challenge, though I shall never get anywhere near the standard of Macaulay's schoolboy. Sparrow told me the other day that G.M. is now pretty well gaga, which causes some confusion in hall and common room. Sparrow is his literary executor, and some years ago G.M. told him to destroy all unpublished writings. I doubt if there are many, but certainly G.M.'s letters should be preserved, and perhaps some published. I have quite a lot.

Jonah was seventy-four last Monday and was much pleased at my sending him a greetings telegram. He will be at the Lit. Soc., and his new book will soon be in proof.

One day I trekked again to Putney and had lunch by Arthur Ransome's bed in which the poor old boy has now been for four months. He's bored stiff, can't sleep and is often in pain: clearly my visits distract and amuse him, but the journey takes an hour each way (with a change and wait on the underground) so I don't go as often as I should.

The Obscenity committee on Thursday held what I hope may be one of its last meetings, for on April 24 our Bill (amended but not disastrously) comes up for Report and Third Reading.

Diana Cooper's second volume is ready and will go to you next week—in time to prevent your being tempted to read the extracts in the *Sunday Times*. Fleming's book comes out a month later. As far as possible we try to stagger the appearance of our more successful books.

The Budget leaves my withers unwrung: I suppose we're all fractionally better off, but it doesn't seem enough to get excited about. Beer I seldom drink, and a commercial-vehicle-chassis plays no part in my life—or yours. The printing strike looms distantly, but I lose no sleep on its account.

15 April 1959   *Grundisburgh*

Your birds, I think, make more of a show than ours do. But have you ever glimpsed a kingfisher? I have *once*, and never again, but once is enough to set one living in hope continuously. And—here is *my* bit of swagger—has your robin ever sat on your mowing-machine *as you mowed*?

Yes, but don't forget R. Birley is a fanatic Oxonian, and wouldn't even admit A.J.P. Taylor to be truculent, or Trevor-Roper conceited. But loth as I am to admit it, I do think O. has something which C. has not, apart from their respective curricula.

I go to Cambridge this afternoon to discuss the G.C.E.—and mainly to say without infuriating them why the other boards have a less civilised approach to examining in Eng. Lit. than the O. and C. which I represent. As it must involve my throwing buckets of doubt on the value of *any* examining on Eng. Lit. I shall, as you see, be treading on thin ice. But I am *always* aware of the wisdom of Jelly Churchill's saying that Eng. Lit. should certainly be taught in school, by those who knew *and loved* it, but never examined on.

Your account of G.M.Y. reminds me of an Eton occasion when the classical pundits, from Rawlins downwards, were puzzled by something in, I think, Tacitus, and someone suggested to Gow that he should put the question to Housman. Gow refused, on the grounds that H. would merely say that the meaning was obvious to the feeblest intellect—and never say what it was. The old curmudgeon!

Jonah was *delighted* by your birthday greetings. He really is rather a disarming old dear; he so loves being kindly treated. Ivor B. was excellent value, and so was Peter F.—an immensely likeable fellow— and no bores darkened the doors. Ivor B. maintained that N. Cardus is not so much deaf in the ordinary sense, but that as he never *has* listened to anything said to him, he now can't! Jonah, alas, was not greatly attracted by the Johnson Club, especially when I told him S.C. Roberts's paper was well above our average. We both agreed on the vast superiority of the Lit. Soc. evenings and also on the major reason, i.e. the greater intelligence, trouble, tact, humanity, spirituality, loving-kindness, and general qualities of body, soul and spirit of the Lit. Soc. Secretary.

Monday morning, 20 April 1959   *Bromsden Farm*

Alas, I must have got up too soon, for the flu counter-attacked savagely and I have been in bed all week-end. Still there, in fact, with some fever. Cannot read or write properly, but will send you a letter as soon as I can.

St George's Day [23 April] 1959   *Grundisburgh*

Stupid of me! Not that it would have made any difference (Ruth did not contradict me when I suggested that, like Winston and in fact all good men, you were a very bad patient!). But if you had used the word *flu* I would have told you what all doctors have said about the '59 germ, viz that it is in itself fairly mild, but convalescence from it is slow. Any number I have met complain that though soon past the worst, they feel second-rate for a longish time. Hope you have a good leech. Mine is a charming man, but I sometimes wonder if it is the *whole* duty of doctors to agree genially with the patient's diagnosis of his case. Still, as a body they have found out so much in the last thirty years as to make it certain that the earth will be intolerably full in twenty years time. Anyway so says Huxley in his revision of *Brave New World, not* a cheerful book! And fancy an accurate and literary scientist misquoting 'And *beer* do more than Milton can To justify God's ways to man.'[1] Do you know the worst misquote in the language? Andrew Lang in his History of English Literature (mercilessly trounced by Henry James) has 'All the charm of all the Muses, flowering often in some lonely wood'.[2] And wasn't he a friend of Tennyson's—who never forgave Sir William Harcourt for referring to his 'earliest pipe of half-awakened birds-eye'? Ivor Brown told me that C.E. Montague often misquoted, and defended himself on the ground that it was pedantry to verify by looking up. I don't agree, do you? The printed word should be as accurate as possible. *You* never pass a misquote in a proof I bet. Pamela is highly appreciative of Diana Cooper's second volume, though she found rather too much about *The Miracle*. I haven't read it yet, but start to-night.

My meeting at Cambridge over the G.C.E. went off all right, though a young bearded highbrow from the north objected to my saying that answers on poetry produced dictated judgments and second-hand raptures (which of course is luminously true, as Gore used to say). How common in matters educational, religious or political is high-minded cant! The young beardie maintained that it is not hard to teach the young how to enjoy poetry. Nor is it—if a teacher is *first-rate*. And how many first-rate teachers are there? I have met four in thirty-seven years—and none of them taught Eng. Lit., which is the hardest subject.

This is an interim report, so to say. More would bring the temperature up again. By the way Pamela, chuckling last night, proclaimed, what no one else has seen, a similarity between Diana Cooper

[1] It should be 'malt' (A.E. Housman, *A Shropshire Lad*, lxii).
[2] All the charm of all the Muses, often flowering in a lonely word.
(Tennyson, 'To Virgil')

and me! Only I fear in one respect, i.e. when Duff was late for something, she was convinced he was dead. I am exactly the same about her or indeed any of the family.

Delighted with your letter to-day. Still bedridden, feverish, unable to read, write or think. Perhaps *jaundice* now plays a part. If I could find the wall I'd turn my face to it like Mrs Dombey. Will write when I can.

There is no evidence that anyone about to have jaundice regards a letter with anything but the same nausea which is instantly produced by the mere thought of eggs and bacon, fried sole, mushrooms on toast, cheese remmykin etc, but there is perhaps the faint chance that it might not.

You would, I think, be incredulous and amused to know how much I hate your being ill. I feel quite inclined to act as old Carlyle did—i.e. sent a bottle of Mrs C's medicine to an ailing friend, having no idea what it was supposed to cure, or what the friend had—an action which he somehow did not think incompatible with his conviction, communicated to a doctor, that a man might just as well pour his complaints into 'the long hairy ears of any jackass on the road' as into a doctor's.

But how is that immense pile accumulating on your desk to be dealt with? I don't suppose I could help, could I? I am at present engaged in writing brief biographies of more or less otiose people like Surrey and Langland and Lydgate. The last, if you please, they used confidently to class with Chaucer. I nearly misjudged Porson when he wrote of Southey's *Madoc* that 'it would be remembered when Homer and Virgil were forgotten', but he regained his pedestal with a bound by adding 'and not till then'.

The ink keeps on drying on this letter, because I am in the summer-house, there is a cherry-tree on my left front, an almond (or is it a prunus?) on my right ditto, and as you know, 'fifty years are little room'[1] to get the full benison of things in bloom; while the sun is out, what *is* there to do but just look? It has been a *good* April, i.e. plenty of rain and not too warm, so it won't upset the summer, or at least oughtn't to. The cuckoo appeared here on the same day as last year, i.e. Shakespeare's birthday—very tentative and his vocal chords clearly needing lubricating. But I suppose you with your nuthatches think very small beer of the cuckoo. Close to he is oddly rough; as the *Irish R.M.* ladies said: 'Not thus does the spirit-voice poise the twin notes in tireless mystery along the wooded shores of Connemara lake,' and even the jaundice-germ must admit, that is a lovely sentence, and Maugham and Murry and Dobrée and Leavis and Orwell (who thought the word 'loveliness' *mushy*) can go to hell. Can you face *music* in bed? It won't do you any harm to sleep as much as you can; you must have heavy arrears to make up.

I liked Diana Cooper's book, though not so much as the first volume chiefly because there are fewer letters from Duff. There are some good portraits in it, and Conrad Russell's letters are good value. He used to come to Tuppy's from time to time, and I loved his slow calm wisdom and humour. Tuppy took him once to dine with a bachelor colony, i.e. Chute, R.A. Young, and Sam Slater. Each came in separately and Conrad afterwards said there should have been some sort of warning, as a guest might easily have a weak heart. They were about as ugly a trio as you can imagine.

I say what an odd and brutal affair U.S.A. law is! That old Sacco and Vanzetti case was bad enough, and now I read that Leopold (who with Loeb murdered a boy for fun in 1924) after thirty years in prison, when his sentence came up for revision was sent back for twelve years. He made good in prison, and did a lot of good scientific work for the U.S.A. in the war. Where is the sense or humanity in that? He was nineteen at the time of the murder and in 1954 had done *twice* as long as an English life-sentence. I wonder what old Judge Wendell Holmes, the wisest of men, would have said.

[1] A.E. Housman, *A Shropshire Lad*, ii.

Now for Ethel Smyth. I have glanced at four pages, and on each there is a row with some very old friend. Why did V. Woolf say she couldn't write? A little occasional loose grammar doesn't mean you can't write, does it? Her two volumes of autobiography are (to me) immeasurably better reading than e.g. *The Waves*. I always, by the way, hated 'Lisl', and expect to hate her more. Nor could I ten years ago do with that fluffy-looking Brewster. E.S. herself I expect to like immensely, though I dare say she could infuriate. In 1879 she was furious with my Uncle Edward for upsetting the cream-jug over Lisl's black velvet dress, and merely saying, 'That's what comes of gesticulating.' Poor U.E. How should *he* know that cream-laid velvet is never the same again?

Shall you manage the Lit. Soc. in a fortnight? And if not how will it survive? If Bernard Fergusson is there let us ask him wasn't Wingate *quite* intolerable as a man. A general nearby says not only that he was, but that his Chindit ventures really achieved very little and used up a lot of men and money. I suppose orthodox soldiers do say that.

4 May 1959   *Grundisburgh*

This is far beyond a joke, even for Nature who loves over-doing things (e.g. drought, rainfall etc). Jaundice is one of her worst ploys— on and on, and human beings share the same pedestal of repulsiveness with steamed fish, which was for days all they allowed me. Not that one wants *anything* much. All summed up in that great sonnet's line 'With what I most enjoy contented least'.[1] The foul thing is just a poison envenoming one's whole body and mind. No chance, I fear, of seeing you at the Lit. Soc. next week. You must have got a very virulent germ at the start. I suppose the leeches do know something of flu by now, and jaundice too. Such ailments as I have are incurable but happily mild. Gow's Itch is one, and the other will shortly be in the manuals as Lyttelton's Finger-Tingle. Gow is an excellent friend to have, because *any* ache or pain one may start he has always had far worse for years and knows all the ropes.

[1] Shakespeare, Sonnet 29.

My letters can hardly help being very dull, because whatever liveliness they may ever have comes from the impact of yours; there is no spark from flint if there is no steel. You must say at once as soon as they show any tendency to turn the yellow ochre of your ailment to gamboge. Do you remember old Johnson's reply to Boswell's complaint that he did not write: 'Do not fancy that an intermission of writing is a decay of kindness. No man is always in a disposition to write; nor has any man at all times something to say.' What even his penetration did not reach to was the man who has nothing to say, but none the less writes, a less common breed perhaps than those who talk without anything to say, but equally calling for suppression. This is of course the age of jaw, and how it darkens counsel. Nothing can happen anywhere without a spate of comment, and when men like Rothermere and Cecil King are at the top, one knows that the comment will be framed to start more comment.

I have just heard from someone who has recently seen Percy Lubbock. He is almost quite blind and longing to be off; but he has a nice young intelligent Old Westminster boy who is a good reader, which makes a great difference to P. My informant, Wilfrid Blunt, says the young man is getting rather a bellyful of Henry James (*The Bostonians* mainly, I think. Is that one of the hard ones? I never read it) and also, inexplicably, Arthur Benson—some of his biographical sketches, no doubt. Not surely *The Upton Letters* etc which, in that nice French phrase, do not permit themselves to be read now. In fact their vogue was gone before he died in 1925. And I imagine E.F's novels and R.H's are as dead as A.C.B's. A very odd brotherhood, so clever, and humorous and self-conscious and ultimately rather futile. The old father must have been a terror, with his temper and insomnia, and intolerance and lack of humour, and religion.

I have just, by the way, finished Ethel Smyth's Life, with great enjoyment. Rather too much about her music and the fuss she kicked up about it, but that doesn't matter, and in all else the excessive old termagant is good fun to read about. The sequence in nearly all her personal contacts recurs regularly—*Schwärmerei*, rage and disagreement, estrangement. I agree with Julia Brewster—the wronged wife—who said 'One has to be very well, Ethel, to enjoy your company' (or words to that effect). It is interesting to read that Virginia Woolf admired her writing (to E.S.) and ran it down to Lytton Strachey. I believe the explanation to be that L.S. was a man with whom communication was apt to have a contemptuous or denigratory tone, particularly about successful contemporaries. Not a really honest man, I put it to you. He admitted that he had no evidence for saying Dr Arnold's legs were rather too short. A small point no doubt, but '*ex pede Herculem.*'[1] But these Bloomsbury highbrows didn't really think any writing good but their own kind, did they?

I have just written brief biographies of Lydgate and Malory. L. is abysmal, M. is sometimes on the *Iliad* level. Why don't you bring out an abbreviated *Morte Darthur*? Perhaps it has been done. Do you know the 'Chapel Perilous' chapter? or 'Balin and Balan' or Lancelot's fight with 'Turquine'? The man—very likely without knowing it—was an *artist*.

10 May 1959   *Bromsden Farm*

I am so touched by the skill and fidelity with which you carry on the rally with no one on the other side of the net. Bless you—your letters are a great joy.

Alas, I am still in bed (three weeks yesterday) and still not fully *compos mentis*. Trying to concentrate for more than a minute or two makes me sweat and feel dizzy. But it's all getting better, and I am far less suicidal. For a fortnight the bemused contemplation of Death—or, as they say nowadays, Total Disengagement—was my constant habit.

Comfort said 'Why don't you read some of your beloved Scott?' But I could face nothing: even a glance through *The Times* reduced me almost to tears (the effort, I mean, not the contents). Now I have got as far as Dorothy Sayers, whose works I am *very slowly* re-reading with much pleasure.

Comfort has to be away teaching most of each weekday, and since there's no one else here she sent an S.O.S. to Ruth, who has been here for the inside of the past two weeks, and returns again this evening. The two of them get on well, so I am wonderfully looked after, and not separated from R.

[1] (We recognise) Hercules from his foot.

Adam has been made keeper of the Junior [cricket side]: when Duff was keeper they won the cup.

Goodness knows when I shall be up or back. We're (R and I) still hoping to take our Yorkshire holiday as planned—but I'll let you know.

In my next letter I'll answer all yours and try to provide better value. This is just to take you my love and tell you that I think I shall survive. The mainspring broke, but the repairers are good these days.

13 May 1959   *Grundisburgh*

Well at least you *are* on the mend, and the really pestilential period is over. Much sympathy was expressed for you at the Lit. Soc. No ailment gets a poorer press than jaundice. Tommy L. says he has had it three times. There was quite a good gathering, just over a dozen. I sat between Ivor Brown and Cuthbert, who was positively sunny. The sun of January rather than of June perhaps, but I am bound to say I found his talk of good astringent quality, and though his valuation of his fellow-men was a long way from being gushing, it was not indiscriminate.

We were in the small room, so there wasn't much *va et vient* afterwards. I had precisely the same conversation with Lockhart that I have had several times, every time in fact before. Luckily I cannot catch more than a word or two, so can simulate fresh interest fairly plausibly. The gist of it is that K.G. Macleod's heart is not what it was; that he is otherwise in good fettle; that with his ability he could have done great things, had he had to, or wanted to; that don't I think he was the greatest athlete ever. I say something about C.B. Fry, he burbles a long sentence of which I glean the gist to be that no, K.G. was the greatest, because he never trained or took any trouble. Here the good Ivor comes trenchantly in and says that is a point in K.G.'s *dis*favour, not the opposite. More burbling, happily *quite* inaudible. It is not you see a thrilling intercourse, but what can I do? I think he supposes that a former putter of the weight is neither able nor willing to talk of anything but the athletic prowess of half-a-century ago.

How immensely encouraging and civilised is what you tell me about Comfort and Ruth happily meeting—the kind of thing that renews one's faith in human nature, which is constantly in need of renewal in a world of politicians and press magnates. (You will not, please, omit to give R. my love.) I found Trollope was the first reading I could face without feeling sick. Tuppy once said a Trollope novel was the best reading in the train, because, *inter alia*, if the wind did blow over a few pages while you took a nap, it didn't matter; you just went on. What was the story about a man who couldn't stop reading a scabrous novel, but at the same time disapproved of it so strongly that he tore out each page when finished and threw it out of the carriage-window? The sort of thing Pepys or Boswell might have done.

In all the letters about Latin I have seen, no one has pointed out that the main reason for preferring Latin to, say, Russian is that half the English language comes from it. In that list of Headmasters in last week's *Sunday Times*, the canvas of the so-called public schools showed them pretty equally divided, roughly all the upper ten (snob!), Eton, Harrow, Winchester, Rugby, Marlborough etc were pro-compulsory Latin, and all the Worksops and Jerseys etc were anti. Not but what some of the stock claims for the study of Latin aren't pretty silly and indeed dishonest. Old A.B. Ramsay somehow managed to persuade himself that it was the *stupidest* boys who got most out of it, which, as the Euclid of my youth used to say, is absurd. But fancy talking of this to one with jaundice!

Roger F. and his wife have just been here—very good company. R. had to supply a brief biography of himself for the back of some Penguin; he will not, I gather, have put in such items as some do, viz Agatha Christie: 'I enjoy my food'—though that appears to be true enough, someone who met her recently reporting that she is enormous. R. is very bad for Pamela, as he often says that we ought all to spend much more money than we do—'every woman being at heart a rake'[1] so to speak. R. has just bought a silk umbrella for £8 odd. So have I—a cotton one costing £1. 15. 0. Do you think my wife is pleased? Not a bit of it—derisive! We took them over recently to see a water-mill of

[1] Pope, 'Epistle to a Lady'.

great age; recently vacated, but leaving on a shutter a number of sea-side picture-postcards which the last miller (obviously a lineal descendant of Chaucer's) had thought funny. So did R. He was particularly tickled by a rustic contemplating two huge show-potatoes labelled 'King Edwards' and saying 'Lummy!—I should have thought they were King Kongs.' It *is* good, as all the rustic was getting wrong was seeing the final 's' in each name as possessive—not plural.

I have read little since Ethel Smyth. I rather liked some quotations from Pfeiffer on old Maugham[1]; 'a good writer of the second rank' is surely right? And the judgment that M's view of life remains what it was at twenty-five is not amiss. And about his friends' visits: 'He looks forward so eagerly to their visits that by the time that they arrive he has had almost enough of them.' 'New friends give him more pleasure than old ones, for they are unexplored territory' was even more pithily put by Tommy L. 'That faint hostility which he calls tolerance.' Who is Pfeiffer?

Whit Monday, 18 May 1959   *Bromsden Farm*

Forgive the biro. I am writing in bed, though since last Wednesday I have been up for an increasing part of each day. That lovely weather was a great help, and I am gradually feeling less groggy and dotty. I sent for all the Wilde material, but haven't yet felt strong enough to tackle it.

Yesterday Comfort and Bridget drove over to Eton and took Adam to see the Duke of Edinburgh play polo in Windsor Park, which they all enjoyed greatly. Ruth and I stayed peacefully here by the fire. On Wednesday morning R. is going to drive me to the sea—probably Brighton or Worthing, where we plan to stay about a week. No rooms are booked, so perhaps you'd better write here, and I'll see that it's forwarded.

Now I'm going to re-read your last *five* letters, none of which has been answered, and will comment here and there.

Most of the time I just slept (one night delirious) and dozed. I had a small radio by the bed, but couldn't bear to have it on. Duff last

[1] *Somerset Maugham, a Candid Portrait* by Karl G. Pfeiffer (1959).

week made 65 not out in twenty minutes for Butterflies v. Worcester. He was dropped in the deep *eight* times (four times by the same chap), and two of the drops ricocheted over for sixes. Today he plays for Fleming v. Nettlebed, and so does Tim. I loved your description of the Lit. Soc.

Next week, stimulated by sea-air, I shall hope to send you a full-length letter. To-day even these two miserable sides make my head spin muzzily. Ruth sends her love—and so do I.

21 May 1959   *Grundisburgh*

What a time you have had! Delirium one night? Did you say the most awful things, as apparently one's subconscious self is a sort of Mr Hyde, and reduces Rabelais to whistle in the matter of vocabulary. Delirious vestal virgins pour out a stream of words they never knew— like the young lady late for dinner, as recorded by Cherry-Garrard illustrating the danger of too great innocence, which I would tell you, if I didn't suspect that I have done so already. Were you prayed for in Henley church? You would have been here; our rector prays for people without being asked to, and once did so for an elderly gentleman who was present, some alarmist villager having said two days before that 'poor Mr Barker had gone to hospital'. And so he had—to have an ingrowing toe-nail dealt with, or something equally un-lethal.

I hope you are past the steamed cod stage in the way of diet, and are on the way to old Heythorp's dinner (Oh no, no R in the month, so no oysters). But you will soon pick up at Brighthelmstone with your lovely companion. (How few people—or drugs!—are *both* tonic *and* sedative.)

I like your tale of Duff's innings on the loveliest cricket-ground in the world—Worcester College. My nephew Charles once hit a ball so far into a neighbouring wood there that it was no good attempting to find it, and no attempt was made. A man *did* go and look for a later hit, and after five minutes a party went out to look for *him*. Charles was a fine hitter and escaped the danger of being caught by an out-fielder by always carrying the lot. There is something majestic about being missed eight times—the sort of thing that used to happen whenever I watched my Junior—when they were in the field. Tuppy wouldn't, couldn't, watch his. He once told us why not. A and B were batting, C bowling. A hit a catch to short-leg (D) and didn't call, so B ran and arrived at A's ground. D missed the catch, but picked up and threw the ball—to the wrong end, where A and B were. B started back to his ground; the wicket-keeper (E) threw the ball to the bowler who broke the wicket when B was still yards away. But he couldn't be given out because there was no umpire, which nobody had noticed. Tuppy added or invented a good many more incidents, but the above ones are *true*. He was quite right—nothing is more degradingly futile than really bad cricket, to play or to watch. I don't mean not very skilful cricket, but cricket not seriously played. Do you know my old friend Harry Altham, the new M.C.C. president? A very good man, excellent cricketer in his day and full of commonsense—an oddly rare combination. He is one of the Governors of North Foreland Lodge girls' school where I (the Chairman) make a speech next week on their fiftieth anniversary. I am in labour with the speech now, but haven't got further than a striking parallel between the present head-mistress and Mad Margaret in *Ruddigore*. As the Bishop of Winchester is also giving an address, I am leaving most of the 'uplift' to him. These occasions are I suppose inevitable but they are none the less dreadful.

I am quite out of touch nowadays. I read *Punch*, *Spectator*, *New Statesman* every week, and I don't understand half what they are talk-ing about, or their comments. So many of the reviewers and com-mentators seem to be intent on a sort of slick profundity. Perhaps they are all very young. I have just got from the library Swinnerton's last novel. Pamela has begun it and says it promises well. Diana last week left behind *Dunkerleys* by Howard Spring and I read it in bed—with enjoyment. It is full of people who are human. Do you put H.S. high? I am a genuine Blimp and ready at any moment to say out loud 'I must say I do like a good story', risking the acid query: 'Why must you say it?' And I am just about to write a thousand words on Chaucer after finishing five hundred on 'the moral' (and intolerable) Gower. I see no prospect of ever being strong enough to tackle Occleve.

I shall have to disgorge five guineas for the new *D.N.B.* volume just out. Do you ever contribute? I was once asked to—about Ranji—

but knowing nothing about his political career in India I declined. Probably I should have come under the lash of that old pedant (was it Churton Collins?) who found over a hundred errors in the first twenty pages of the volume he looked at.

Foully cold to-day. I doubt if you are bathing. Here we *always* begin May with a dazzling week, and follow it with a North Wind full of spikes, and lingering like an unloved guest. I am, so to speak, only just in the summer-house. The Yank family is ensconced over the old stables. Very friendly and happy. P. told them the orchard was the children's playground, but they never go near it, preferring the dusty little yard giving onto the road. I asked the four-year-old why they didn't go into the orchard and got the answer: 'There's chickens there; they might bite me.' Like giving a child a really fascinating toy. After two days it is again concentrating all its interest and affection on a faceless doll, or battered bar of wood, or tailless rocking-horse that doesn't rock.

Get well at once please, Rupert. Breathe deeply, eat heavily, sleep deeply, and don't dream of dizzying yourself with writing a long letter. Love to Ruth. I hope she rules the convalescent with a rod of iron—beautifully camouflaged in velvet.

25 May 1959   *Dudley Hotel, Hove*

Your splendid letter reached me this morning, and I read it aloud to Ruth on the promenade, to both our delights. The improvement in my health is startling. Last Wednesday Ruth drove me the ninety miles from Bromsden (in constant rain) and I was quite exhausted when we arrived. This hotel, though wildly expensive, is thoroughly comfortable, with masses of delicious food. We have a charming room on the top floor, with our own bathroom. The weather has steadily improved, and yesterday (a scorcher) we both *bathed*! The sea was *icy*, and we stayed in for seconds only. On Satu~ lay we spent the afternoon watching Sussex v. Glos and were impressed by Parks, J. both as bats-man and wicket-keeper: also by the batting of Lenham, a gainly young man with a fine free style. One of the umpires was Fagg, A., who, you will instantly recollect, is the only man to have scored two double centuries in the same first-class match.

I am allowed to eat anything, but forbidden alcohol for three months.

I don't think I've ever read anything of Howard Spring's. Life seemed too short. Nor have I ever contributed to the *D.N.B.*, though I suggested many revisions (which he made) in Michael Sadleir's article on Hugh Walpole (in this new volume) and in Harold Nicolson's article on my Uncle Duff (which will be in the next). Here I am slowly re-reading E. Blunden's *Cricket Country* with much enjoyment. You must have read it: do you remember the wonderful description of the household of the Hon William Somebody (the book is upstairs)? Answer this question.

On Thursday we shall reluctantly drive back to Bromsden, so write there, and I shall hope to answer in a letter of normal length.

Who would have believed that Dulles's death could cause all this brouhaha? Will the Court go into mourning when Selwyn Lloyd shuffles off this mortal coil?

27 May 1959   *Grundisburgh*

Good! But I am not surprised: I thought the presence of Ruth would do what no leech with his potions could manage. But no alcohol for three months is rather severe. I don't remember that twist of the rack when I had the damned thing. But as so often happens, one suspects that the faculty doesn't know all that about an ailment. Otherwise why should they differ so much as they do in the treatment? The doctor I had at Eton in the nineties had one treatment for practically everything, 'a hot bath and a hot drink and get to bed', and his patients did just as well as anybody else's. In those days we had 'growing pains' which ascended the hierarchy in succeeding years as rheumatism, lumbago, fibrositis and slipped disc without anyone discovering the cure for any of them.

Cricket Country of course I know, and possess, though where the heck it is now who can say? Books do hide themselves uncannily.

I wonder how old Ivor B. will do at Malvern. I have warned him of the twittering vapidities of the school play on the evening before. I suppose Salathiel Pavy[1] must have played Lady Macbeth and Desdemona adequately somehow, but girls playing men make me shudder. Their thin little voices! Sir Anthony Absolute I remember sounded like an angry starling. We shall see.

There was a lot of absurd fuss about Dulles. A year ago we all said (rightly) what a stubborn old nuisance he was, and now we slobber bibfuls about him. I am reading Gunther on *Inside Russia*. *Most* interesting. Not too much politics and economics, and what there is I skip. Do you realise there is *no* golf-course in all Russia, and that a hat costs £14 and boots £70?

Can you face the printed page yet? Pamela was a bit disappointed with F. Swinnerton. Too complicated, she said. I shall take it to Eton on Friday, my H.Q. for North Foreland Lodge on Saturday when I face the monstrous regiment of women. One story I shall tell which they will like. Do you know it? The girl who had the question 'Where are elephants found?' She had no idea, so wrote: 'Elephants are enormous and highly intelligent animals and are very seldom lost.' But I often suspect you know *all* my stories. How kind you are about them! Love to Ruth. Some things however well known and established must none the less always be expressed. Taking divine and other blessings for granted is one of humanity's worst stupidities.

29 *May 1959*   *Bromsden Farm*

I think the only way of sending you a full-length letter this week is to make it a serial and write a page a day. Ruth and I drove back from Brighton yesterday, your letter arrived punctually this morning, and then Ruth drove home to Hampstead. I miss her dreadfully, but we shall be reunited on Monday, and on Friday there are all the joys of our mountain-top before us. We bathed again on Wednesday: the

---

[1] Boy actor of Shakespeare's time. Ben Jonson's epitaph on him contained these lines:

> Years he number'd scarce thirteen
> When Fates turn'd cruel,
> Yet three fill'd zodiacs had he been
> The stage's jewel.

water, I daresay, was just as cold, but it didn't seem so, and I'm sure that after a week or so I should get quite used to it. We enjoyed the whole Brighton trip enormously—excellent hotel, wonderful weather, no hurry or stress or nuisance. Physically I feel fine (and am so sunburnt that no one will believe I've been ill), but mentally I'm still fairly woolly, and good for only the shortest spells of reading or writing. I have no doubt that this long and enforced rest-cure was badly needed.

Duff has just rung up cheerfully from Oxford. He and seven other drybobs (all members of the college rugger fifteen) managed to pass the necessary scrutiny and are rowing in Eights Week as Worcester IV. They scored a bump on each of the first two days, but are now in the exhausting position of sandwich-boat, having first to row through at the head of their own Division and then catch the tail-ender of the Division above. This looks like being beyond them, and on Saturday (Duff says) they may well get bumped themselves by B.N.C. IV. Have a look at Monday's *Times*.

As a result of our drives to and from Brighton (by different routes) I have firmly decided that I abominate all buildings erected since 1820, and particularly those of this century, ending up with rows of squalid little bungalows that look like insecure anchors for their clusters of television-masts. How comparatively charming and unspoilt the countryside must have been in your youth.

Yesterday Diana Cooper signed copies of her book at Hatchard's, and five hundred copies were sold! Apparently Evelyn Waugh escorted her there, extremely tipsy, and bullied everyone who came into the shop to buy a copy and get it signed! Now I shall relapse into coma and write more tomorrow.

Sunday evening

We were just sitting down to supper last night when Fred's Dame rang up to say that Adam had got a fast ball in the mouth while batting and had been taken to hospital. Later we got on to the hospital and learnt that he had lost one of his front teeth (he had particularly nice ones), poor lamb, and this morning he was reported otherwise all right, except for a bruised and swollen lip. As I have often said before, if it isn't one thing it's another! So far Adam's side have won all three

73

of their Juniors, scoring altogether 460 for the loss of eight wickets: he seems destined to be involved in high scoring, and I only hope this accident won't affect his nerve.

3 June 1959   *Grundisburgh*

It looks as if, fundamentally, Nature or Fate has done you a good turn, viz in making you stay out substantially before you broke down from overwork, as you very well might have. And, dash it all, am I wrong in supposing that it wasn't all worth a week with Ruth? And your northern mountain-top just round the corner. I see it is to be un-settled to-morrow in the north and fine in the south—in fact I suspect a heat-wave, as there invariably is when I go a long train-journey with a heavy suitcase. Ivor B and I go to-morrow to Malvern. He sends me a mysterious postcard saying he will probably be joining my train at Evesham—where, if I remember rightly, it doesn't stop. I used—*aetat* thirteen—sometimes to watch the expresses thunder past Slough, and —I think—the South Wales expresses do ditto past Hagley, and merely swelled with pride when my father stopped our train from Eton at Hagley, which normally it ignored. He was a director of the G.W.R. and had a gold token on his watch-chain which enabled him to travel first-class, free, all over England.

North Foreland Lodge no longer plays cricket, and in the absence of Harry Altham I congratulated them on dropping it and likened women's cricket to what Dr Johnson said of women's preaching.[1] I am not sure they didn't think I was referring to Dr Hewlett Johnson,[2] and not Dr Samuel. The Olympic fencing champion was there, an N.F.L. old girl called Gillian Sheen. She is a professional dentist, and the N.F.L. fencing instructor gravely told me that the wrists which brought her fame in *l'escrime* must guarantee outstanding certainty and despatch among the molars and bicuspids.

I see Duff's pessimism about what would happen on Saturday was, alas, justified. A sandwich-boat has a hard time. My junior four at

[1] 'Sir, a woman's preaching is like a dog's walking on his hinder legs. It is not done well; but you are surprized to find it done at all.'
[2] Popularly known as the 'Red' Dean of Canterbury (1874–1966).

Eton was never as high as that; they had their work cut out usually to keep away from the Maidenhead pleasure-steamer. In a rowing manual I once glanced at I read that there are twenty-eight possible mistakes in putting the oar into the water, i.e. even more complicated than the golf-swing.

How right you are about the countryside. I remember how I used always to feast my thirteen–eighteen-year-old eyes on Oxford as the train approached it—and me a fanatic supporter of Cambridge—and it really is heart-rending to think what Oxford must have looked like a hundred years ago. What with the gasometers and Nuffield and the traffic, it is mere hell in August now.

I hope Diana Cooper's book is filling the firm's coffers. The reviews I have seen are good, though of course the *New Statesman, more suo,* has to have its little sneer. Who the devil is Eisenstein who gets a full page in the *T.L.S.*? Pryce-Jones seems to be deliberately making it less readable week by week. But John Carter was good on some egregious Yank professor who seems to have been tampering with Housman's text in a manner which would have burst H's gall-bladder. I cannot imagine what the man will say in reply.

I *am* sorry about Adam's front tooth. It is another black mark against a drought that school-cricket pitches are all horribly fiery, and the parched earth is sprinkled with front teeth. W.G's famous ball from the Australian Jones nearly did the same; after all the beard is only an inch or two away.

On Monday I go to Oxford (c/o R. Mynors Esq, 14A Merton St) and on Wednesday return here. Your address is locked in my bosom. I shall not be sorry to miss the Lit. Soc., *te absente,* and so avoid the censure of Sir Cuthbert.

8 June 1959   *Kisdon Lodge, Keld*

Although I'm writing this on Monday I fear it can't reach you till Wednesday—if then. Our faithful farmer will take it down the hill this evening and it should leave tomorrow. I'm addressing it to Grundisburgh for safety.

My three days in London last week seemed very hot, exhausting and *noisy* after my six weeks in the country. I played about in the office, saw as few people as possible, visited Arthur Ransome in hospital and dined quietly with my father at the St James's Club. There I saw Osbert Sitwell, terribly shaky now with *paralysis agitans* but still just able to eat and drink without help. I gossiped agreeably with him for a little.

The Fourth of June seemed endless. I borrowed my sister's car and at 11 a.m. picked up Alistair Cooke, Eric Linklater and wife, Duff and a girl. Mercifully no rain fell until the last half-hour of the Fireworks. Comfort brought a magnificent picnic of cold chicken and strawberries. Also a splendid new gadget (I think American), a bag which you can fill with ice and bottles. Adam, gap-toothed but cheerful, met us carrying his home-made radio, from which the Test Match commentary was issuing. Comfort took Alistair to see School Yard etc while I watched the cricket, and tried to avoid seeing too many friends, for I soon began to feel dizzy and tired. I did however see Jonah and Evy, John Carter, Peter F. and a few others. Another picnic for tea, more cricket-watching, then an excellent dinner at Monkey Island, though I began to long for an alcoholic restorative. Alistair never stopped talking for a second all day, which was an enormous help and enabled me to remain mum. By the time I had dropped them all and got back to Soho Square it was 1 a.m. and I was too worn out to sleep. However the thought of coming here sustained me through everything. On Friday Ruth and I lunched with my sister in Hampstead and then drove off happily. We had tea in Northampton and stayed the night at Bawtry, just south of Doncaster. That left only a hundred miles for Saturday, and we were in the cottage by 3 p.m., having been driven up the hill with our luggage by the farmer's son in his jeep. His wife had already swept and aired everything and lit a magnificent fire, so we settled in immediately. That night we slept eleven hours, and last night the same. The climate here is quite different from anywhere else. Ever since we arrived a gale has been blowing, with intermittent sun, and we are glad of a fire in the sitting-room all day. We also have a delicious one in the bedroom in the evening. The place is alive with curlews and larks and on the last stage of our drive, coming up the pass from Wensleydale, we saw our first blackcock—great excitement. I have brought the Eddie Marsh biography[1], and on the shelf *How Green was my Valley* awaits me. Otherwise it will be mostly Oscar.

If A.E.H. had destroyed all his scraps, drafts and manuscripts, instead of leaving them to his asinine brother Laurence (whom he despised), none of what Carter rightly complains about would have happened. I see P. Lubbock is eighty: I must write to him.

Ruth has arranged lovely bowls of kingcups and wild geraniums, the grandfather clock ticks peacefully, the wind howls outside, the view is unbelievably beautiful—we are in paradise.

10 June 1959   *Grundisburgh*

I returned here this morning and your letter arrived this evening— the posts of course being cleverly arranged so that one can't answer till the next day. You don't sound all that well yet, but I hope that a spell at Kisdon Lodge will so work that you tread the ling like a buck in spring.[2] Of course the Fourth of June has often reduced men of conspicuous eupepticity and vim to the last state of Augustus the chubby lad.[3] Not since I was a boy do I remember thinking it anything but a day of wrath. It does go on and on. The longest reach is between tea and dinner, or used to be; it was always then that the most boring Old Boys called and simply would *not* go. How would you feel now if a real bore appeared at 6.15 and cheerfully announced straight away that he 'needn't leave' till 8.15, as his party wouldn't be back till then? I gather they have restricted the number of firework-tickets so as to keep out those rowdies who used to turn up tight and throw things about. There is no human being I detest more than the fourth-rate Old Etonian. It was this kind of thing that put an end to Montem,[4] and I have often hoped that June 4 might go the same way. After all

[1] By Christopher Hassall (1959).
[2] Kipling, 'The Ballad of East and West'.
[3] After refusing food for four days:
> 'He's like a little bit of thread;
> And on the fifth day he was—dead!'
From *Struwwelpeter* (1847) by Heinrich Hofmann (1809–1894).
[4] An Eton festival which took place every year from 1561 to 1847.

why make such a fuss of George III? Where did I recently read a demure reference to the undoubted truth that the only Kings of England that were certifiable were the two with whom Eton is most closely connected?[1]

I have a fancy you had *How Green* last year, but never quite got to reading it. I hope you will. The Welsh idiom, to my ear and mind, is as entrancing as J. M. Synge's Irish. There are too some grand scenes and people. I fell without a struggle in love with Bronwen and have never fallen out.

Ivor Brown did very well at Malvern. In the train thither his external appearance was much as you describe. I noticed that his aquascutum (wholly superfluous as the day was hot) was frayed, and gaped in a good many places, but on speech-day he was in spotless dark blue, and they all thought his appearance was most distinguished (it *is* a good face don't you think?). His speech to school and parents was *excellent*; he did not depend as so many do on a handful of funny stories (there were one or two of course), but the serious passages were in exactly the right key, and so well phrased that every ear in the audience was alert: I think he enjoyed the whole thing; he was certainly given a very warm welcome by everyone, old and young.

The book I had with me on all these journeys (Bromsgrove at the week-end) was your uncle's *Talleyrand*. Has it ever been fully appreciated? It seems to me beautifully done. How did he thread his way through the hideous tangles of French Revolution intrigues? T. seems to me a really great man in many ways—so far-sighted and sure in all his counsel, which the little cad of a megalomaniac[2]—so like Adolf H. in many ways—after a time ignored. I am about half-way through.

On Monday my old pupil John Bayley and his wife Iris Murdoch came to dinner. I liked the tousled, heelless, ladder-stockinged little lady—crackling with intelligence but nothing at all of a prig; her only defect as a dinner-neighbour was a too low and rapid utterance. My daughters of course say their father is as deaf as a haddock, but it wasn't only that, as the other guests agreed about her inaudibility.

[1] Henry VI, who founded the school, and George III, who was born on the Fourth of June.
[2] Napoleon Bonaparte.

Douglas Veale, the ex-Registrar, claimed to be the only Certificate-examiner whose report had been quoted in *Punch*. He had referred to a 'howler' in a Latin Composition paper, and Graves or someone got hold of it. A boy putting into Latin 'the more I do something or other, so much the more wine I drink' wrote '*eo plum vinum bim*'. He is a charming man and lunched the Abbey School Governors royally—smoked salmon, roast duck, strawberries and cream, plus (or plum) a courtly and consequential hock, and a raffish, anecdotal brandy, to borrow from an old vintner's catalogue.

How right you are about A.E.H. and his folly in leaving his stuff to a brother whose brains he openly derided. Old Gow, who had *some* say, but not much, told me he had great trouble with Laurence, who had *no* discrimination, and A.E. knew it, but none the less left him to print what he thought good and burn the rest. As Gow acidly said, L. didn't know what *was* good. What I find annoying is that so little of A.E's admirable prose survived. He wasn't going to trust anyone with that; one lecture he actually tore into tiny fragments page by page, as he delivered it. The pedantic old churl didn't choose to leave behind him anything not perfect, and, despising the judgment of his fellow-men, he was unmoved by their praise. He was curiously humble about his English prose. All he said about such things as his superb address when George V visited Cambridge was 'It may have a certain amount of form and finish and perhaps a fake air of ease, but there is an awful history behind it.'

15 June 1959   *Kisdon Lodge, Keld*

Your spanking six-pager was brought up the hill by Mr Hutchinson, the faithful farmer, and has given much pleasure. A week here has made all the difference to my health, mental and physical, as I knew it would, and I now feel perfectly well, with another blessed fortnight stretching ahead. The browsing and sluicing might not be to your taste, but they suit us fine. Take yesterday for instance—a heavenly day with fourteen hours of continuous sunshine from a clear blue sky. We got up at 8 (an hour earlier than usual) and breakfasted behind the cottage on the eastern side. Two upright garden-chairs and a pretty portable table. Invariably our breakfast consists of cornflakes (which I never touch elsewhere) with brown sugar and fresh farmer's milk, bread, butter, marmalade and tea. Then I smoke one of the four pipes to which I ration myself each day—large ones, you know, stuffed with strong flake tobacco (Erinmore and Condor Sliced) which I smoke only here. Then, yesterday, we sat all the morning reading, sunbathing, and watching a pair of curlews keeping guard over four mobile babies in the grass. Lunch, also alfresco, consisted of a delicious veal, ham and egg pie which my sister had sent from some special place in Nottingham, with salad, followed by white peaches (from a tin) washed down with lemonade. By mid-afternoon the sun had moved over, so we shifted chairs and table to the front of the cottage, where we can contemplate the extravagantly beautiful view. Tea, out there, is all of the farmer's wife's baking—fruit-cake, shortbread and ginger-biscuits, all first-class. About seven we came in, lit the fire, and at 8 had our accustomed supper of boiled eggs, lemon-curd tart, bread and jam, fruit and Wensleydale cheese, with more tea. Then we draw up our armchairs to the fire and, with the Aladdin lamps on the table behind us, read and gossip till bedtime. I have been concentrating on Oscar, but have also re-read Evelyn Waugh's first book *Decline and Fall*, which is still very amusing, and am plodding through *Eddie Marsh*. I should say two hundred pages could have been cut with advantage. There's a lot of interesting background stuff, but one longs for a bit of foreground, which the impotent old ninny is too dim to provide. It's small beer in a gallon pot, but I shall persevere to the end. *How Green* still beckons from the shelf!

Reverting (as they say) for a moment to browsing, Ruth is always longing to cook elaborate meals, but I won't let her (though she's a wonderful cook) because I want her to have a proper holiday. I relent only on some Sundays, when we have hot meat and occasionally sausages.

So glad Ivor was a success at Malvern: I felt sure he would be. I agree about *Talleyrand*: for a first book it's an astonishing performance. I brought it to Jonathan Cape soon after I arrived there, and its great success did me a lot of good.

You will be pleased to hear that Oscar is at last on the move again, and by the time we leave here (alas!) on the 29th he should (E and O.E.) be ready for the printer. But what use is that, when every printer will be on strike? God knows how long it will last, but it's sure to cause a sickening hold-up in our business.

This morning I have, from the back window, been watching a wheatear feeding its young. I even photographed the operation, but Ruth says it won't come out because of the reflection of the window-pane. We shall see. At the moment R. is upstairs, giving the bedroom a vigorous spring-cleaning. We have fetched the water from the spring and washed up the breakfast things. It's a beautiful day, but so far with little sun, and our fire is already lit (I having cleared out yester-day's before breakfast). I tell you all these domestic details so that you can get some idea of our idyllic existence. Sometime between 5.30 and 7 this evening the farmer will come up to milk his cows, bringing us our letters and Saturday's papers, which we shall read after supper, taking the *Times* crossword in our stride. To-morrow we may possibly go shopping, as it's market day in Hawes, and if we get another scorcher like yesterday we shall drive to the east coast for a bathe—probably to a charming little Victorian watering-place called Saltburn-by-the-Sea, north of Whitby. We've been there once before. To our disappointment there haven't so far been any local sales, but we shall get the local paper this evening. Now I must turn again to Oscar, and soon it will be time for lunch.

18 June 1959   *Grundisburgh*

Lovely! Just what I wanted. I now have the picture of you both pretty clear, and only a snapshot of the countryside—which I don't suppose for a moment you have—is lacking the full-length. The brows-ing does sound just right; I assume you have your eye on the veal and ham pie's successor. Also that you are in the land of baps and ban-nocks, or failing them, what John Buncle called 'extraordinary bread and butter'. (It is much the most absurd book ever written.)[1] The

---

[1] *The Life of John Buncle, Esq.: containing various Observations and Reflections made in several parts of the World, and many Extraordinary Relations* (vol I 1756, vol II 1766) by Thomas Amory, an eccentric Unitarian who was married seven times and died in 1788, aged ninety-seven. Hazlitt called him 'the English Rabelais' and Leigh Hunt published extracts from his work in *A Book for a Corner* (1851), but all agree on his absurdity.

curlews were a nice touch. I hope you agree the ginger biscuits *must* be Huntley & Palmer's. They are Medes and Persians at my table and always have been. (No, I re-read and see that yours are home-made. That is all right, provided you give *no* encouragement to imposters like McVitie & Price.) But one does have shocks. I once met a man who *preferred* shredded marmalade to Cooper's—which is putting Eddie Marsh above Augustus the physically strong, who reverberates through Carlyle's Frederic (always so called). Your supper is the very spit of ours pretty well every Sunday.

That you *still* haven't begun *How Green* cries to Heaven. I suspect you know you won't be able to put it down if you start. Perhaps you will when I tell you emphatically that Ruth is in it all right—not of course the only book where she is.

Granny Gow has just been here for a long week-end, rather too long! He is very infirm and can't do practically anything for himself. And daily becomes more inaudible—he just can't be bothered to speak up.

We have reached the strike season. Already four or five in progress. There is nothing which shows up the folly of *homo sapiens* more clearly. How shall you fill your working hours? What about that book you ought to be writing? Have you dipped into the new *D.N.B.*? It is much less impersonal than the old ones, and Leslie Stephen's motto 'No Flowers' is fairly often ignored. So far it has not had a very good press. There was a silly slating by R.H.S. Crossman in last week's *New Statesman*—so smug and cocksure and Wykehamist—complaining that craftsmen and socialists in industry were inadequately treated. Is the *D.N.B.* meant to be a history of the times? He admits that there have been very few outstanding socialists. I cannot see that Maxton and Ellen Wilkinson are very poorly handled. What, after all, did they *do*?

I am lost in admiration of anyone who does the crossword 'in his/her stride'. I never do it, partly because I don't as often as not understand the clue. I never was the smallest use at any kind of puzzle. Monty James always had a huge jigsaw going; it made me tired to look at it.

I heard from Percy Lubbock to-day—quite a cheerful letter to my surprise. He seems to have plenty of company, and I gather friends played up well for his birthday. That *T.L.S.* man hinted there might be too much Pater in his style. I don't see it. I am not well seen in Pater, but seem to remember that his self-consciousness was nearly always perceptible, and I see no sign of it in *Earlham*. I confess I found P.L's *Edith Wharton* hard going, but largely because I disliked her so much. I suspect Henry James was much tried by her. Gow hates H.J., particularly *The Turn of the Screw*, which he calls an 'obscene' book. And one can't call him exactly prim. I suspect it frightened him, as it well might. Butterwick began it and didn't dare go on. But he always had the liver of a chicken, though a good man at Sotheby's. The book that terrified *me* sixty years ago was *Dracula* and I believe still would; and I didn't much want to read *Uncle Silas*[1] in bed. I once read at Eton a ghost story called 'Thurnley Abbey' to a lot of boys in a room lit by one candle. Some were very pallid when the lights went on. Do you know it?[2]

Eighty-three in the shade! 'Rich and deep was the day, gathering its power, bending its great energy to ripen the teeming garden' (*Earlham*, of course).

Good to hear you are *well* at last. But how could you *not* be with that nurse?

22 *June 1959*   *Kisdon Lodge, Keld*

I meant to devote all yesterday to my blest pair of sirens, George and Oscar, but the unbroken sunshine of the longest day kept me outside, where there was just enough breeze to make writing tiresome. So I fear this will be a day late.

So glad you approve of our feeding arrangements. When I get back I shall hope to send you some snapshots of our miraculous countryside, but they are difficult to take: we are so perched up that the perspectives go awry and spaciousness becomes a huddle. Still, we are persevering with Ruth's new camera.

[1] By Sheridan Le Fanu (1814–1873). Published in 1864.
[2] By Perceval Landon (1869–1927). Published in his *Raw Edges* (1908) and reprinted in *The Supernatural Omnibus*, ed. Montague Summers (1931).

On Saturday night our farmer cut the hay in the fields before and behind us, so now instead of waving flowers and grasses we are surrounded by the delicious smell of new-mown hay, freshened this morning by some heavy rain which fell in the night.

Granny Gow sounds an intolerable visitor: thank God we haven't got him here! In fact we want no visitors at all, and even resent a passing hiker miles away. I completely agree about R.H.S. Crossman, though maybe he does you good by releasing a flow of adrenalin into the blood-stream.

Have I never before mentioned crossword puzzles? I'm sure I must have, for they are almost the only things I am (through long practice) extremely good at. I began doing them when I was at Eton, which is also when *they* began, and have done *The Times* one pretty well ever since (it used to be difficult to get hold of when I was a private soldier in barracks in the Blitz). Normally in Soho Square Ruth and I do *The Times* one in ten minutes or so during our morning coffee. I also do the *New Statesman* and *Spectator* (have won thirty shillings' worth of book tokens this year so far), the *Observer* (Ximenes) and the *Sunday Times* (Mephisto), but the best of all is the *Listener*, which is often most ingenious and amusing (occasionally it becomes mathematical and I retire). Luckily Ruth shares this passion, as she does everything else. We both love jigsaws too, but they take up too much time and space.

On Saturday, a perfect summer's day, we drove twenty-three miles across the moors to Barnard Castle, where we shopped. Then on to a sale in the Temperance Hall of a nearby village. We stayed only for the china and oddments, which took one and a half hours, and bought three plates, part of a charming tea-set, an engaging toast-rack and two lovely coloured lithographs in maple-wood frames—all needed and suitable here—for a total cost of 14/9. (There is another, nearer, sale on Thursday.) We drove home through Teesdale (which you would think beautiful if you hadn't seen Swaledale) and over the moors again to Brough on the edge of Westmorland.

I haven't shaved for over a fortnight, but alas the growth is slow, and I still look more unshaven than bearded. What there is is a pepper-and-salt mess, though Ruth sweetly says it's getting golden in the sunshine. I long to see what the finished effect is like, but in another week it will all have to come off. Have you ever grown a beard? It's delightful not having to shave I find.

I see much more Henry James than Pater in Percy Lubbock's style, and I never got right through *The Region Cloud*[1]—did you? I too loved *Dracula* in my youth, and at home I have a fine first edition (quite a rare book): I must try it again. *Uncle Silas* I have never tried.

Yesterday, when I meant to be writing to you, I finished *Eddie Marsh*. I think you'd better put it on your library list. It *is* too long, and E.M. is more pathetic than heroic, but there are lots of good jokes and stories in it, and it's generally entertaining. Quite a lot of Winston. The account of Rupert Brooke's last days and death is graphic and moving.

Ruth has gone out to pick wildflowers, which she arranges in heavenly little bunches all over the cottage. You've no idea how pretty cotton-grass can look. The orchids are over, but any amount of other things are in flower.

We might possibly come up here again for a week or two in August, if I have the face to absent myself even *more* from the office. The strike has pretty well brought work there to a standstill, they tell me, and I see one optimist forecasts that it may last for *ten* weeks!

Ruth has just come back with masses of orchids (not over at all!), wild geranium, sorrel, vetches, grasses and bluebells. She sends you her best love and says she particularly enjoys the flattering references to her in your letters.

25 June 1959   *Grundisburgh*

I returned this morning from my girls' school, where every year I behave for two days exactly like that hearty old horror Mr Chips. The dreadful thing is that I much enjoy it, for, like the dear Doctor, I dearly love a knot of little misses. I have two granddaughters there— fourteen and eleven, who luckily don't take after their grandfather in looks, and are great fun. The headmistress has a touch of genius. She once got a lot of small girls to write down anything they thought or

[1] Percy Lubbock's only novel.

wondered about the headmistress's ways, and more than one apparently asked 'Why, when short skirts are the fashion, does Miss X always wear long ones?' She laughed delightedly and said: 'But don't you realise that I have such hideous ankles'—i.e. she has like Monty James so much natural dignity that she never has to stand on it. The assistant mistresses are always the slightly disheartening element in a girls' school. Why must so many of them be so *anaemic*?

I return to a garden the colour of the Sahara, or at least the Gobi desert—and in Hampshire yesterday there was half-an-inch of rain and all the madder-browns were emerald-green in twelve minutes. What does 'madder' mean? and, if it comes to that, why crimson *lake*, burnt *siena*, and yellow *ochre*? As far as I remember, crimson lake had the nicest taste, and gamboge—why *gamboge*?—the nastiest, perhaps because so much yellow comes from arsenic. Every hour or two the fire-warning goes, as some heath catches fire from a cigarette-end, or even from the rays of the sun concentrated through a lemonade-bottle. The Lord Cranworth, who knows our climate intimately, says it may not rain till October—as in 1921 when the barley was eighteen inches high. Couldn't you *bottle* some of your new-mown-hay fragrance and send it here?

No, Granny Gow would *not* do at Kisdon, though you would enjoy his dry flavour in the right surrounding. After all, even Housman produced a silvery laugh after punishing the Trinity port laid down in Edward FitzGerald's time. A tight smile was all I ever saw. And how right you are on the flow of adrenalin. The health I have is largely due to Leavis and Amis and Osborne and the *New Statesman*, and the umpire who gave me out in a critical school-match at Eton.

My respect for you and Ruth, which might have been thought incapable of increase, approaches the region of awe at what you tell me of your crossword powers. It is tremendous. I can't believe it is only practice. There is native genius in it somewhere. Ximenes! A friend staying here once took fourteen minutes to get *one* word—and that turned out to be wrong. Will you do the *Times* one in my presence one day? I shall feel like E.V. Lucas watching Cinquevalli[1], i.e. seeing things done which he *knew* to be impossible.

---

[1] The great juggler. See volume one of these letters.

I saw Harry Altham yesterday—actually cheerful about modern cricket! There were 32,000 spectators at Lord's on Saturday. I said—following an august example—'What went they out for to see?'[1] The answer was not John the Baptist but May and Cowdrey. To which *I* reply: 'That is not enough; in my day there were at least twelve to see, in a Test Match, perhaps more.' But H.A. is famous for euphoria and eupepsia (and eugenics too; he has a *cold* bath every morning, and when I asked him if he bathed in the Serpentine in January, his negative was not emphatic. But in spite of these drawbacks, he really is the nicest man you could want).

Pamela's mouth watered at your sale exploits, and mine did and does at the name Swaledale. It *must* be lovely, isn't it? Or is it like the Black Country where the names Daisy Bank, Cradley Heath, Windson Green have been given to a series of down-at-heel slums and slag-heaps (not that the names approach the broad and opulent majesty of Swaledale. I like writing it and rolling it round the tongue).

Yes, *The Region Cloud* is unreadable. I don't think I ever arrived at any notion of what it was supposed to be about. You *must* read *Uncle Silas* at night, by the light of one candle, preferably with a wind moaning round the house. I notice a suspicious silence about *How Green*. How well I know that state of affairs. Have I praised it too much? That fatal treatment has kept me off any number of books, e.g. Damon Runyon and Thurber.

I grew a beard in Greece in 1912. It was *red* and far from popular. No one ever said anything as nice about it as Ruth did about yours. But then—no, better not. I shall say it some day when she isn't by!

29 June 1959   *Kisdon Lodge, Keld*

We have stolen two more days here, and will now drive south on Wednesday morning. My colleagues report a complete stoppage on account of the printing strike, the redecoration of my flat (bathroom and kitchen) won't be ready till Wednesday, and Oscar was within two days of being ready for the printer. Luckily to-day and yesterday have been cool and wet, so I am full steam ahead with him, and by Wednes-

---

[1] *Matthew*, 11, viii.

day he will be printer-worthy. There are still a great many missing notes, dates etc, which I hope to gather while the type is being set up —and it's possible that a few new letters may turn up—but the major work is done, and the relief enormous. While we've been here I've transferred thousands of corrections (on 850 letters and 1600 footnotes) to the top (printer's) copy, so now we have a complete duplicate of everything. *Laus Deo!*

While I am writing this, Ruth is engaged, three foot away, on a fascinating task. We have a little folding card-table, which is useful indoors and out. Its green baize top was full of holes and very shabby, so we cut it off and bought some new scarlet plastic material which has to be ironed on (through brown paper) with a hot iron. We have a splendid iron, given us by our farmer's wife (who is now all-electric): it consists of an ordinary iron-shaped container and handle, inside which one puts a chunk of iron, heated red-hot in the heart of the fire. Irons in the fire at last! R. has now done the top of the table beautifully, and is struggling to iron the edges at the side and underneath.

For lunch we had lettuce sandwiches, Wensleydale cheese, apple pie and stewed gooseberries. My beard has another day to live: R is now rather taken with it, saying I look like a sea-captain. A suitable photograph will be taken.

I wish you could see the great stretches of green which sweep away from us on every side, topped by the heather-covered fells. No Gobicolour here. (By the way, Peter F. told me long ago that the word Gobi means Desert, so Gobi Desert is a tautology: I love pointing out such pedantries to one who enjoys them.)

Next time I visit you I will do *The Times* crossword in your presence: it's sure to be an especially difficult one, and I shall be humbled.

We went to another sale last Thursday—an enchanting one out of doors in a little village. We bought (for a total of 24/9) a coloured china rolling-pin, a very pretty candlestick, two sweeping-brushes, a double saucepan, a first-class Aladdin lamp with shade (one of ours was a bit dicky), and a lovely glass plate engraved with dates etc of the 1887 Jubilee. This last will probably come to Soho Square and be proudly shown to you.

Ruth has triumphantly finished ironing the table, which looks splendid.

I'm not sure whether you realise that Keld and Kisdon are in fact *in* Swaledale, which stretches from here to Richmond, without benefit of railway. It is far the loveliest of the Dales: I'd love you to see it, but we could get you up here only in a jeep or Land-rover.

Next week-end is Long Leave, *and* Henley Regatta, *and* Adam's sixteenth birthday. All he wants, he says, is a new slide-rule, which he must choose himself.

Duff is going to Greece with David Caccia (Harold's son), but I don't know what he's going to use for money.

Ruth is now settled by the fire with a book from the cottage library —*Hetty Wesley* by Q. We have a fine run of Nelson's admirable seven-pennies—much better print and binding than our vaunted Penguins. My reading has lately been all Oscar, except for a chapter or two of *The French Revolution* at bedtime. I am still only just over half-way through, and Dogleech Marat is scarcely on the scene.

On the table is an exquisite bowl of wild roses, which R. picked yesterday in the rain. Both the last two nights we have slept for *ten* hours! I send all these details so that you can a little picture the scene. As I finish each section of Oscar, R. reads it through to see what I have missed; she also types many new notes, which I cut out and stick into the bulging folders. No one else will ever know *quite* how much work has been involved.

The drive on Wednesday—a melancholy business—will take us eight or nine hours, and we shall hope to start about mid-day, after packing up and stowing away everything here. Two days in the office, and then Bromsden Farm, where I shall eagerly expect your letter. Comfort reports a garden as parched as yours, and there will be almost a month's accumulation of bills and other horrors to tackle. I take it you will be at the July Lit. Soc.—and beforehand in my attic? It's the last dinner before October, and somehow I shall have to get through it on barley-water. Up here we never drink any alcohol anyhow, so the prohibition is no trouble. Now I must polish off Oscar, and then it will be tea-time, and then we shall cross two fields to fetch a pint of fresh milk and this morning's post, including Saturday's newspapers. It's a perfect life for us.

Write to me, as Oscar says, when you have something better to do.

Thank you for your note about Gobi. Why is nearly all the information one picks up inaccurate? Only recently someone (R. Mortimer?) applied that lovely sentence of Gibbon's 'Twenty-two acknowledged concubines . . . ' to Commodus instead of Gordian. Cousin Oliver reported his father's eulogy of *W.G*'s neck. Well I don't suppose the doctor's rivalled driven snow, but in sober fact the remark was made about E.M's.[1] When a fourth leader repeated the canard I wrote a brief correction which they have ignored. Housman always maintained that a love of truth was the rarest of human virtues. I am much enjoying Peter's Boxer book.[2] It surely deserves the good reviews it is getting. And your uncle's *Talleyrand* greatly impressed me. How *did* he find time to acquire that mass of facts, sift them and present them with a confident lucidity which makes the book delightful reading?

How grumpy you must be feeling, having exchanged Swaledale for Soho Square (*I* feel grumpy in sympathy!) where I suppose all is in a sort of chaotic idleness. The lay view, at any rate in Suffolk, is that workers who strike for a huge advance when their wages are already much higher than most people's, must be in the wrong. The man Briginshaw's face has the same stolid and irascible mulishness as that of 'Terrible Ted' Hill of the Boilermakers. But I understand very little of what goes on. Nobody seems to share (e.g.) my bewilderment at Cousins and his damned union solemnly pontificating about nuclear bombs. They can of course give their opinions as individual voters, but why as an industrial body? Especially when one knows that not one in twenty has given more thought to the pros and cons than I have to gynaecology—not so much in fact.

I remember the 1887 jubilee (*aetat* four), or rather I remember two things about it (a) that I contributed a spadeful to the planting of the Hagley Jubilee oak, and (b) that I was shortly afterwards sick—thus contradicting the common fancy that one always remembers pleasant and forgets unpleasant things; for I have no recollection of the delectable comestibles that had that lamentable result.

---

[1] E.M. Grace, brother of W.G. and like him a famous cricketer.
[2] *The Siege at Peking* by Peter Fleming (1959).

Christopher Hollis came here to give away the Woodbridge prizes. He did it very well in a crackling voice, though stressing rather unnecessarily at one point that all his audience, old and young, were born in sin. I don't think Woodbridge parents hold any such view. They look rather what one of the old Forsytes termed a 'rum-ti-too' lot, resembling in fact to my eye the sort of crowd one sees in January in a bargain basement. If you say that merely shows I have a good deal of 'snob' in me, I cordially agree with you. But there it is.

I hope you didn't miss that review (some good man, but gosh! my memory in 1959!) in which a good deal of praise of the E. Marsh book was tempered by a remark that it compared unfavourably with the Life of Hugh Walpole. This is not *nearly* well enough known. However, you can say with Landor: 'I shall dine late but . . .[1]' Readers' tastes are unpredictable and who knows that better than you? Surely Oscar W. will bring the shekels pouring in. I am full of excitement about it.

I remember reading *Hetty Wesley* years ago and have a vague memory of an iron upbringing—e.g. flogged for crying after a flogging, surely a good example of the vicious circle (the best example perhaps is that of the man whose soup was so hot that he sweated into it, and it increased in such heat and quantity that he sweated even more. Not a very delicate instance perhaps but cogent). The 'dog-leech' episode I remember as wonderfully vivid, in his 'slipper-bath' whatever that may be. How sporadic and local your uncle shows the 'Terror' to have been, daily life in most places going on much as usual. Perhaps all revolutions are like that. Marat I imagine as largely lunatic. Does Belloc write of him at all—as he did, splendidly, about Robespierre— 'a man all convictions and emptiness, too passionless to change, too iterant to be an artist, too tenacious to enliven folly with dramatic art, or to save it by flashes of its relation to wisdom.' Isn't that pretty good? (but I wish I was *quite* sure what he means by 'iterant').

Not much of a day—hot sun and wind, a poor combination rivalling, no doubt feebly, the Gobi Gobi. Swaledale is the place. Your little saga of it—last four letters—is full of music, say Beethoven's

[1] '. . . the dining-room will be well lighted, the guests few and select.' To which more than a century later W.B. Yeats added, in 'To a Young Beauty':

> And I may dine at journey's end
> With Landor and with Donne.

'Pastoral', and Ruth stars it like that lovely air that recurs throughout the second movement (do you boggle at 'stars'? I mean it as Conrad uses it 'the channel glittered like a blue mantle shot with gold, and starred by the silver of the capping seas'), and though you use practically no adjectives her presence graces every little picture you paint. What fun—and frequent pain of course—it must be to be an artist!

P.S. Have just acquired an Irish linen jacket. Pamela says she has waited forty years to see me well-dressed.

5 July 1959   *Bromsden Farm*

It is ten p.m. and I have just come back from driving Adam to Eton —a long stream of almost motionless cars most of the way—after what must be the sunniest and hottest Long Leave for many a year. I have been in the garden, exiguously dressed, catching up on four weeks' worth of everything. All now happily disposed of, thank goodness.

Those last two stolen days in Swaledale advanced Oscar most satisfactorily: two pouring days of rain, on which I copied and composed while Ruth checked and typed beside me. And then on our last day the sun returned, and we went for a last lingering walk along the top of Kisdon: soft turf studded with wild thyme and many other flowers, curlew calling, an occasional grouse or hare. That evening the farmer took down the hill in his jeep (with the milking pails etc) four large parcels of books and typescripts, and in the morning we got up at 8.30. Packing up the cottage and stowing everything away took $2\frac{1}{2}$ hours, and then we walked sadly down the hill laden with haversacks and carrier-bags. The drive to London (265 miles) took us nine hours, including substantial halts for picnic lunch and tea. As usual London seemed stifling, ugly, crowded, and above all *noisy*. Soho Square, which nine years ago was delightfully quiet at night, is now pandemonium until 1 a.m. at earliest.

I love your liking all the Kisdon details (the snapshots should be ready tomorrow), and if Ruth shines through them like a star, that is exactly what she does in my life. When the time came, on the last evening, for the beard to be removed, R. became quite sentimental about it. Incidentally I had a fiendish time getting it off.

Fleming's book is selling splendidly, but we shall run out of stock if the strike goes on more than another fortnight. Briginshaw (as you unerringly sensed) and his union NATSOPA (which, by the way, my daughter was forced to join when she went to the *Farmers' Weekly*) are easily the worst of the lot. That union contains all the *un*skilled workers in the various trades—hewers of paper and drawers of ink—and they are constantly trying to get as much money as the skilled men. The only advantage of the strike is that no proofs can arrive to demand my attention, and in a few days my desk should be clear.

Only yesterday did I see that review which praised my book at the expense of *E. Marsh* (it was by Angus Wilson)—very gratifying, I must say.

Adam's side is in the semi-finals of the Junior, and their hopes are high. The only year Fred won the cup was when Duff was captain of the side! At the end of the half Fred is moving to the new house, which seems to be slap in the middle of Judy's Passage. Goodness knows how one will approach it with car and luggage. It has central heating, Adam says. His new (temporary) tooth is so lifelike that I couldn't tell which it was.

On Friday night we all went to an excellent entertainment in the grounds of our neighbours the Brunners (Lady B. is Laurence Irving's sister); with lights, recorded music and voices they told the story of a tragic pair who were imprisoned in the tower there for the murder of Sir Thomas Overbury. All very well done, and *delicious* sandwiches (some of creamed haddock, some of chicken and mushrooms) obtainable from stalls manned by devoted women slaving for the Village Hall.

I see that Suffolk is beset with heath-fires: I hope they're well away from Grundisburgh: I don't want you singed.

Oh yes—among the massed correspondence here I found a rebate note saying the Inland Revenue owe me £193!! Another Eton half assured. I go from hand to mouth.

9 July 1959   *Grundisburgh*

It is quite infuriating but I cannot manage the Lit. Soc. on Tuesday. Those bovine and malignant G.C.E. authorities have piled on to me a great mass of scripts—far more than they had led me to expect—and no more time in which to get them marked. So I simply cannot spare a day and a half while they silt up. I was greatly looking forward to it, and especially to a good crack with you. Really the cussedness of things!

London, poor you, must be quite ghastly in this heat; and any thought of Briginshaw must damp your forehead. It does mine here! I like, or rather I don't like, the simple reactions of him, Cousins and their kidney. 'We don't like arbitration because the case for a strike is always so weak that the arbitration invariably goes against us.' Damn them all.

Good news about Adam's tooth. In old days it would have been dead white, i.e. matching no tooth that ever was; in still older ones the gap would have been irreparable. And just think what dentistry must have been in Dr Johnson's day.

I am writing a life of Shakespeare in 1500 words for Dick Routh's wildly improbable biographical dictionary. I don't find it very easy. Until I really began to poke about I hadn't realised how very few facts about him are really known. The point I have arrived at combines the convictions that W.S. of Stratford couldn't have written the plays, and that no one else could have. You may remember that old Agate, after toying with the Baconian theory, came, characteristically, to the conclusion that S. wrote the bulk of every play but that he was Bacon's 'fancy boy' and his patron put in numerous odd bits here and there. But does that really hold more water than any other theory? It is interesting to find that Masefield found in the Stratford bust 'a man with much vitality of mind' and that the Droeshout portrait, which most people find frankly doughy, shows 'a face of delicate sensitive-ness'. Isn't this wishful thinking? I shall of course give Tolstoy's opinion; after reading all the plays some seven times he says that the universal admiration of the poet proves the world to be mad.

I much enjoyed Peter's book. He gives the whole Boxer affair the right tone of fundamental absurdity punctuated with horror. I love the explanation of the rebels always firing high as they thought the higher the rifles' sights were set, the more potent the shot. I hope the six hundred millions of them are equally childish now. There are grim possibilities about a people who don't value individual life waking up to the truth that collectively they can overwhelm the rest of the world.

Yes, I remember, it was Angus Wilson, one of those (to me) immensely clever and entirely unreadable novelists—but evidently a first-class critic. The Library is being very dilatory about the Marsh book, but it doesn't much matter as I spend much time daily getting up the answers to the G.C.E. papers next week. Many of the questions are much too hard for sixteen-year-olds, viz 'What does *Pilgrim's Progress* gain by being in the form of an allegory?' (Don't breathe this to anyone! The paper is to be done next Wednesday.) And now candidates like John Betjeman's daughter will turn out a brilliant answer of breath-taking fulness. I often find that several candidates are both cleverer and more learned than I am. I except the Barbados boy who wrote 'Wellington was the French general who helped Nelson to defeat Napoleon at Trafalgar Square.' And I did *not* invent that.

Adam appears to be always leading his side to a crushing victory, whatever the game. He should be comfortable in the new house—overlooking my old garden. In 1895 at Benson's we had one bathroom, candles, no heating, but a very large number of cockroaches. One always appeared whenever I had a bath.

How long did your beard get? Could you curl it? I remember the agony of removal. I believe there is a convenient technique, but never knew it. And isn't your skin very tender underneath? We are of course really *meant* to be bearded.

12 July 1959   *Bromsden Farm*

It's very sad that I shan't see you on Tuesday, and Ruth will be as disappointed as I am. Never mind—we must look forward to October. Meanwhile, here to divert you, are a few wholly inadequate photographs of Kisdon. Next time we shall try to take some that will give you a better impression. Be an angel and let me have them all back. I can't tell you how I yearn for that company and landscape. If I hadn't all these children and other responsibilities, I should leave London and publishing, fame and fortune, and fly to Swaledale. 'Dark and true and tender is the North.'[1] However, things are as they are, and for the nonce I must hang on, hoping for a few more blessed days in August. Anyhow the piloting of Oscar through the press will take a full year. I am even now drafting the introduction and am truly on the last lap, though I keep on finding hideous mistakes. Ruth says this is bound to happen in so large an undertaking and I mustn't worry: we shall pick up all the errors in the proofs: I hope she's right.

Last week in London was too much of a good thing, and on Wednesday night I lay sleepless and gasping on my bed, with all doors and windows fixed open to admit the roar of engines and the cries of roysterers. Now it is mercifully cooler after much thunder and rain, and I hope it will keep so while you correct those numberless papers and write your life of Shakespeare on a threepenny-bit.

Certainly the Lit. Soc. wouldn't have been much fun last week. Next Sunday I'll report on Tuesday's dinner. I don't in the least mind my liquor-prohibition, but it makes other people's drinking seem unduly protracted and boring, and I can quite see why teetotallers so easily turn into prigs.

On Thursday I lunched with T.S.E. to discuss the London Library, whose A.G.M. is on Tuesday. He was suffering a little from shortness of breath, but was most genial and charming. I am quite devoted to him: he is a saintly character but entirely human, with an unexpected sense of humour. He explained gravely and sadly that his false teeth didn't allow him to eat his favourite raspberries in public. I have always preferred older people to those of my own age or younger, and I dread the time when I am left the oldest.

I fear Adam isn't as good at cricket as Duff was, and he got no further than the XXII. But luckily Adam has a happy accepting temperament and doesn't worry about such things.

I am *still* reading *The French Revolution*, and have now reached Part 3: *The Guillotine*. I keep that here, and in London am reading a huge tome called *La Jeunesse d'André Gide*, which is surprisingly interesting, and right in the Oscar period.

I wish I liked Lord Birkett. He is that frightful thing, a professional after-dinner speaker, full of smug clichés. He is much disliked by his brother-judges. Perhaps he'll be able to get some sense into these

[1] Tennyson, *The Princess*.

bloody printers. Meanwhile all is at a total standstill, and I have almost caught up with my arrears of correspondence. Some say that when the strike is over, all the printers will take their fortnight's holiday, but I find this hard to believe. They'll surely be short of money for one thing.

Snapshots returned, with many thanks. Interesting to see that Nature meant you to be a blend of Ezra Pound and the late Kaiser Wilhelm II. I get a delightful impression of Swaledale and your 'settled low content' which is Orlando's fantastic phrase for a pleasant humble abode. All the candidates write practically the same answers about *As You Like it*. The teaching of Eng. Lit. is now dreadfully competent as regards attaining a decent pass-mark, and beyond that very prosaic and boring. The fact is that teaching in Eng. Lit., to be any *real* good, demands a spark, and sparks are just as rare in Academe as anywhere else. But there is definitely something charming about these snapshots coming while I am at this play, for there is a congruity between Swaledale and the forest of Arden. I am not *quite* sure whether to see you as Jaques (you are looking *very* thoughtful), Orlando, or the Duke. There is no difficulty at all about Rosalind. You know, my dear Rupert, the Swan of Avon frankly maddens me at times. I have had to look into *Much Ado* again. Do *you* find Beatrice the last word in charm? I don't believe it. I am sure Ruth never tricks and twirls the language about like that! It is S. the *poet* who appeals to me; the dramatist is so wildly silly sometimes—simply could not be bothered; e.g. in *As You Like It* Orlando not recognising Rosalind in the forest, and the fantastic pairing off of Oliver and Celia. Apropos of the former, some great detective once said that anyone could disguise his or her face, but the voice was very difficult and the walk still more so. It was this last, wasn't it, that dished Miss Le Neve on that ship. Or was it her shape, for I believe the captain said much the same of her as Sainte-Beuve said of George Sand, viz 'She had a great soul and a perfectly enormous bottom'? I always felt sorry for Crippen; he had tremendous courage and the day before his death wrote a very good letter to Miss Le N.

Did you know that when the search for him was on, and his picture was everywhere, some Etonians got hold of a photograph of Michael Bland[1] and sent it up to Scotland Yard? There was certainly a strong likeness.

You interest me about Birkett. The fashion is to say he is splendid. I heard him give a good literary lecture once, and he likes watching cricket, so he cannot be all bad. He is or was a much nicer man in court than that coarse and truculent Patrick Hastings was. I never met him, but once, as someone's guest sat near him at lunch at the Garrick. He was being very crusty about his food. I was lunching with old Pellatt[2], and on our way out he had a brief chat with Seymour Hicks, who said more really witty things in a shorter time than I have ever heard. Pellatt said he was always like that. If I lived in London that is the club I should like—and should probably be blackballed for it, as old Agate was. I think that was one of the few things that he felt permanently sore about. I can imagine that a 'queer' who had to pay away hundreds a year in blackmail would not be *persona grata* to a good many members.

I haven't seen what happened at your London Library meeting. Who *was it* who said to me recently that 'if anybody can defeat the Inland Revenue it will be R.H-D', but he was not optimistic. I am afraid they win much more often than not. Shall we ever see T.S.E. at the Lit. Soc. again? By an odd coincidence, it was only a week ago that my sister-in-law refused a plateful of raspberries and cream on the same grounds. But surely dental plates should be more pip-tight than that? I wear a plate, but gollop raspberries whenever opportunity offers. Mouth-roofs of course vary. A leading retired general near here cannot find a plate which does not cause him acute agony whenever inserted. He will have to get his gums like those of Caesar's soldiers, i.e. hard enough to bite anything after the teeth had worn away.

How long is your liquor-embargo to last? Old Heythorp in his prime wouldn't have stood it as long as you have. I wonder why you don't mind more.

Do you know anything about one Paul Johnson, deeply dyed in the *New Statesman* colours? In a recent article he had the impudence to

[1] Eton master.
[2] Headmaster of a prep-school.

reproach the Queen for attending a race-meeting while Parliament was discussing those Mau-Mau floggings. Can stupidity and malice combined do better than that? I see your supporter Angus Wilson says he is going to vote Labour because his family's Toryism infuriates him. It seems a poor reason. But almost every day something in the papers sends my temperature soaring. I wonder if there will be any papers soon. I doubt if Birkett or anybody else will do much. Why do I associate printers' holidays with a mysterious word viz 'wayzgoose'? I must look it up again, -nth time.

P.S. I have rheumatism in the left wrist and am shortly to have electric treatment from a man called Prodger—a name straight out of H.G. Wells or Dickens.

19 July 1959   *Bromsden Farm*

I can't resist sending you Adam's last letter (please return it). I particularly like 'the maddening crowd' and his modesty in explaining that the wicket was easier when he went in.[1] Now, on the strength of his performance, Adam is playing in the final of the House Cup, where Wykes's are again the opposition, and sound likely to win.

This weather suits me fine, except in London, where it is hellish. All this week-end I have been in the garden wearing bathing-pants and basking. Only nine turned up for the Lit. Soc. and we dined in the small room. Contrary to all tradition, Tommy insisted on my sitting on his right. Jonah has recently had pneumonia, but seems little the worse. We had *consommé en gelée*, cold duck with orange salad, fruit with ice-cream, and a cheese soufflé. I ordered a huge jug of iced barley-water for myself and got through pretty well, though I was delighted to go home at 9.30. I find prohibition no worry at home, but it seems to make me tire easily in company.

Your experience correcting papers on Shakespeare reminds me of the days when I stood at the back of the Old Vic stage, carrying a

[1] Coleridge's won the Junior Cricket cup by an innings and 92 runs. They scored 156 to their opponents' 38 and 26. Adam made 43 and took 7 wickets for 4 runs.

halberd and wishing all Shakespeare was as good as the best. For instance, the three casket scenes in *The Merchant of Venice* are almost intolerable to listen to, night after night. All I can say for Beatrice and Benedick is that when Gielgud and Diana Wynyard played the parts they seemed very witty, but at no other time. You're right about Seymour Hicks: he was always wildly funny, and in the Garrick took as much trouble with the dimmest young new member as with his own cronies. The Garrick is very hot against homosexuals (though one or two have slipped through): they say it isn't so much the chap himself as the sort of friends he's likely to bring to the club, and some knowledge of the Savile, where there is no bar, makes me think they're probably right.

The Annual General Meeting of the London Library passed off smoothly. T.S.E. presided with grace and grave charm. A tiresome old fellow called Waley-Cohen said he'd taken a book out of the Library which was full of anti-French propaganda, and would we please return it to its publisher. I told him we couldn't be responsible for the contents of all 750,000 books in the library, but that I would 'look into' the matter. Our rating appeal has now been put off till the autumn. We lodged it more than a year ago: the law's delays do not grow shorter.[1]

I haven't yet got to the execution of the King, but the pace is quickening, and I know the best is still to come.

You are right to associate wayzgoose with a printer's holiday, since that is exactly what it means. This year I hope it chokes them.

Apart from the resultant financial loss, and the certain prospect of a frightful scrum of books in the autumn, this period of stagnation suits me very well, since it is enabling me to tie up innumerable loose ends in Oscar before he goes to the printer. Last week I got *eight* new letters: none of surpassing interest but all worthy of inclusion. The total is now well over 900.

[1] In 1957 the London Library, which had for eighty years been immune (as a charity) from paying rates, was suddenly informed by the Inland Revenue that it would in future have to pay £5000 a year. An appeal to the Lands Tribunal was dismissed, and when in October 1959 the Court of Appeal upheld that decision, the Library already owed the Inland Revenue upwards of £20,000. Hence the immediate appeal for money which is mentioned later in these letters.

So sorry to hear of your rheumatism: Prodger sounds just the chap for it.

Tomorrow evening Ruth and I are being taken to Gielgud's Shakespeare recital. I'm pretty sure I shall enjoy it, since he does all the best bits, and his verse-speaking is always a joy.

I wouldn't at all mind seeing Olivier's *Coriolanus*; I've never seen the play acted; but the journey to Stratford and the need to book tickets months ahead rule it out. Olivier, to my mind, has no idea how to speak verse, and never will have, but he has other qualities, and I don't care what anyone does to *Coriolanus*.

Did I tell you that Comfort is going to France with her mother for a fortnight on August 11? Adam goes to stay with friends in Scotland on the same day, and we're hoping to nip back to Swaledale for ten days or a fortnight. It depends on the strike, the office, my partners' holidays etc. So far I haven't liked to raise the question, so soon after my long absence.

I can't pretend I'm mourning that foul-mouthed old horror Munnings:[1] his conversation in the Garrick was like a stopped-up-drain released, and I'm not at all interested in horses.

23 July 1959   *Grundisburgh*

I don't see how this is to help being a scrap, since mainly through the incompetence of the G.C.E. pundits at 'the older and more splendid university' I have been sorely pushed these last few days. And I was just hoping that the work this morning would go on wings, when I came upon thirty papers on *Eothen*[2] done by young women who knew the book by heart and rewrote most of it with astounding speed and disheartening illegibility. So I have again fallen behindhand, and to-morrow the worst paper of all comes in—nearly three hundred of them. This was the paper last year which produced *forty-eight* sides from John Betjeman's daughter, who was at that convent school at

[1] Sir Alfred Munnings (1878–1959), President of the Royal Academy from 1944. Painted mostly horses.
[2] *Eothen, or Traces of Travel brought home from the East* (1844) by A. W. Kinglake (1809–1891).

Wantage where apparently it is *de rigeur* to write about three–four words a line in enormous handwriting. It is almost impossible to mark with any confidence an answer that extends to eight pages; one has forgotten the beginning as one nears the end.

A near neighbour of ours who lost her husband very suddenly a month ago had her house burnt down on Tuesday—'Father-like He tends and spares us.' Nobody knows why, though wiseacres are pursing their lips and shaking their heads over a Russian maid, 'a chain-smoker of cigarettes' they say. The next house to this one has a thatched roof, and the owner of it and his wife are always in a dither about fire. I suppose you saw about the train which puffed fifteen miles to Felixstowe, followed by a fire engine. Pretty well every yard of the banks on the railway from here to London is black. And the heavens are as brass.

A lawyer friend of mine won't have it that they don't like Birkett, and wonders where your information comes from; he says if B. cannot patch up the strike, no one can. Is there a more up-to-date text in the Bible than 'Jeshurun waxed fat and kicked'?[1] The worker has plenty of money now, so goes on insolently demanding more—and good men like you and Christopher Hollis are heavily mulcted.

The Lit. Soc. dinner sounds very toothsome—but you don't say whether it was wild duck or the tame villatic fowl: I suspect the former as you mention orange salad. I don't like your still being on the waggon. All wrong. How long, O Lord, how long? The body 'that handful of supple earth and long white stones with sea-water running in its veins' may be a thing to marvel at, but it goes wrong too easily and too often. Prodger's ante-room is a 'sair sicht'. I am easily the most lissom mover.

Of course you are right. Shakespeare needs to be *acted*. Beatrice and Benedick I do remember liking years ago, at Birmingham if you please, where they don't act as well as D. Wynyard and J. Gielgud. D.W's sister was gym-mistress at the school where Diana and Rose went and got all D's old clothes. The real surname is Cox, which is harmless. In my youth there was a pin-up called Olive May; her surname was Meatyard. Names are fearfully important. Just imagine if *Paradise Lost* had been written by Hobsbawm.

[1] Deuteronomy, xxxii, 15.

I too shed no tears over Munnings. I met him here shortly after his famous Academy speech. He went on with it interminably, and (like his speech) without a happy turn of phrase, or scrap of wit anywhere. A tedious old man. Talking of the foul-mouthed, I have just read the life of Frank Harris.[1] Max B's cartoon of himself and F.H. at dinner is the best thing in the book. Have you read his autobiography? Unprocurable by the layman, but I always imagine publishers can get anything they want. Do the Yanks allow it? I see some old Judge in U.S.A. has just been very broadminded about *Lady Chatterley*, which, apart from what George Forsyte called 'the nubbly bits', seemed to me a tremendously dull book. But I have never been able to do with D.H.L. Bedside reading *pro tem* is D. Henley on that dreadful old virago Lady Carlisle.[2] All the worst Victorian *grandes dames* rolled into one, with an extra pinch of temper, snobbishness, and intolerance.

I was stung on the lip last week by a wasp in my port, lunching at the Cranworths'—ten minutes after old Lowther—Speaker's son— had been stung by a different one in *his* port. A completely unique incident. For the next twelve hours I resembled the late Ernest Bevin.

26 July 1959   *Bromsden Farm*

I do hope Prodger will cure your rheumatism. Seventy-six is no age these days, and I thank Heaven that you are otherwise flourishing. My old friend Arthur Ransome (whom I visited at his Putney home last week) has been bedridden for seven months with some kind of rheumatoid arthritis. He is seventy-five, and I begin to fear he will never walk again. So does he, and the other evening, when his wife was out of the room, he said in a woeful voice: 'I'd always hoped to end respectably.' His wife, a large and vigorous Russian woman of sixty-five, refuses to have any kind of 'help', and the task of nursing, cooking, cleaning, shopping etc is clearly wearing her out. It's all most distressing, but my visits seem to cheer them up and I am going again soon. The journey from Soho Square takes an hour each way, unless I

[1] By Vincent Brome (1959).
[2] *Rosalind Howard, Countess of Carlisle* [1845–1921] by Dorothy Henley (1958).

hire a car (which I did a fortnight ago, dreading the heat-wave rush-hour in the Underground). It took half an hour and cost 24/-.

My information about Birkett came from a Judge of the Appeal Court, but let it pass. Perhaps the old boy will settle the printing strike in the end. I fear the Lit. Soc. duck was tame—so sorry! Where does the 'handful of supple earth etc' come from?

I'm sure that long ago I told you of the collection of bad and funny book-titles made by me and William Plomer in the 1930s. I've just found a new one for the collection—a slim volume of Nineties verse called *Vox Otiosi* by David Plinlimmon. Can't you see it? And how well the title would suit a thousand other books!

Last Monday Ruth and I were taken to John Gielgud's Shakespeare recital, which proved to be an evening of rare pleasure. Wearing a dinner-jacket on an empty stage surrounded by red curtains, he recited and acted many of the loveliest speeches, interspersing them with Sonnets, and with extremely apt comments of his own on what was coming next. It was wonderful to hear a whole evening of S's supreme poetry, without any of the boredom and nonsense that so often intervene. He spoke all exquisitely, so that one heard and understood every syllable. I wish you could have heard it. Afterwards we supped with the great man at the Ivy. He was in excellent form and most amusing. When I commented on his admirable restraint in Romeo's balcony and death scenes, he said: 'You've no idea how much easier it is without a Juliet. When there's a beautiful girl above you on a balcony, or lying on a tomb with candles round her, naturally the audience look at her the whole time, and Romeo has to pull out all the stops to get any attention.'

My dictionary says that the origin of Wayzgoose is 'obscure', and it's not in Johnson. I'm sure that tiresome fellow Eric Partridge would have an opinion ready. But Ivor B. is your man.

Last week I also visited Donald Somervell in the Queen's Gate Clinic. He has had part of one kidney removed and is now undergoing four weeks of prostrating ray-treatment. It sounds terribly like cancer, but he was very cheerful, reading a life of Cardinal Manning by day and P.G. Wodehouse in the evening. I said I'd go again next week. Luckily he has a nice woman-friend to look after him.

So sorry about your lip, but if you *will* dine in noble houses these days, I suppose you must expect the port to be full of wasps. Believe it or not, I am *still* battling with Oscar, finding more and more that needs doing. You'll certainly waste some days when that comes along! I've no evening engagements next week, thank goodness. London buildings are not organised for heat-waves.

30 July 1959   *Grundisburgh*

You mustn't be compassionate about my paper-markings. No schoolmaster is so resentful of drudgery as other human beings. A lot of rot has been poured out. The pay isn't all that meagre, and the woman who said her husband had been sacked for making a mistake of half a mark in eight hundred papers was—in Swift's courteous phrase —saying the thing that was not. I have in fact had two grimmish days —fifty-seven scripts from Downside, where the young papists, know-ing, like Father Brown, the paramount necessity for obedience, had learnt their five books practically by heart, as no doubt they had been ordered to, and wrote volumes of decidedly stodgy but undeniably accurate and comprehensive information. I felt definitely grateful to the occasional one who wrote a few pages of scanty drivel—and of course to the one who wrote lyrically of Keats's unsurpassable adjec-tives, e.g. '*bearded* bubbles winking at the brim'. What I, as an exam-iner, call a really good school is e.g. Clayesmore, where their answers are like the prayers of those who mourned Sir John Moore—'few and short'.

Prodger's efforts are so far as unavailing as the tears and sighs of the ungodly, filled with guilty fears, who behold His wrath prevailing —an awfully silly line surely? If God is omnipotent he could have easily made them less ungodly, and if omniscient why that outburst of angry rage? Really Hymns A. and M. *are*! But Prodger is quietly confident; he has the air of a sworn tormentor of old who knew that if his thumb-screw didn't make much impression his rack certainly would. My doctor hinted the other day that at seventy-six one must not expect aches and pains to vanish as they used to, and that I am very lucky, especially as internally my heart is like a rainbow shell that paddles in a halcyon sea.[1] When are you going to be let off the waggon? That is a much more serious affair. And it looks as if after Bank Holiday your nose will once more be to the grindstone; no doubt Wayzgoose will prevail over the week-end. I am glad, by the way, it *was* a tame duck—much more toothsome eating than wild, though I believe one mustn't say so. I don't know where the 'handful of supple earth' comes from. I happened on it as *quoted* by Rider Haggard. It is less contemptuous than Webster's 'a box of worm-seede at best'.[2]

That Gielgud evening sounds fine. This morning I hear from Routh who too was there, and echoes your praises of it with a few grace-notes of his own thrown in. He says that he *and* his two neighbours (hard-faced city men, he says) were *all* in tears at the *Lear* passage. I like to remember that old Johnson, when editing Shakespeare, refused to read *Lear* again, as he simply couldn't face it (or 'up to it,' as *all* G.C.E. candidates say, as well as 'meet up with' etc. What the *hell* are their English teachers doing?). Routh also says that he came away convinced of the *extraordinary* beauty of *All's Well*. So I am again wrong. Minorities usually are ('About things on which the public thinks long it commonly attains to think right'. Dr J. may be taken to apply to Shakespeare). That is an interesting remark of Gielgud's about *Romeo and Juliet* and manifestly true. I suppose he has thought out everything he does. Do they all? I remember Agate recording how he complimented Benson[3] on some inflection or gesture, and B. candidly said he had merely done what he did without thinking. But no doubt lots of the big things in words or action are instinctive. What news of D. Somervell—though they do take a kidney out for other reasons. But those who know always pull a long face if they hear of deep-ray treatment. I do hope he will be all right. Prodger, if you please, had half his lung removed last winter; that *was* cancer, and he is quite sure it came from smoking cigarettes. But he is *very* cheerful—and optimistic.

Nice little silly joke—Parson to choirboy mentioned ethics. Boy looked blank. 'Don't you know anything about ethics?' Boy: 'No, Sir; I live in Thuthex'. Sorry!

[1] Christina Rossetti, 'A Birthday'.

[2] *The Duchess of Malfi*, act iv, scene 2.

[3] F.R. Benson (1858–1939), Shakespearean actor. Knighted 1916 on the stage of Drury Lane theatre.

It is Bank Holiday morning, eleven o'clock and all's well. Yesterday I spent entirely in the sunny garden, occasionally nipping indoors to provide Oscar with another or a better footnote. Ever since I got the top copy of the typescript ready for the printer, more and more things have turned up demanding additions and alterations. Also I am finding, just as I did with *Hugh Walpole*, that the books one read at the beginning of a five-year job yield a lot more if re-read at the end. One doesn't completely know what one's looking for until the work's in final shape. How bored you must be with all these minutiae of editorship—and how little the results will be noticed by most of the book's readers! Though, in fact, good editing, like good printing, should be so suited to its subject as to be taken for granted.

Several of our main printers are on holiday (wayzgoose to you) till today week, and we shan't get much out of them till the end of August. Ruth and I are hoping to nip up to Kisdon on the 12th or 13th for the best part of a fortnight: exact details next week. My American friend Leon Edel, the Henry James expert, arrived with his wife last week. They are spending a month in England, based on Ruth's house in Hampstead.

I can't follow Routh's remark about *All's Well*, since it didn't figure in Gielgud's programme. Someone has blundered. J.G. has certainly thought out and perfected every syllable and gesture: did you read that interesting interview with him in Friday's *Times*?

I spoke to Donald Somervell again on the telephone. He sounded much better, and is now spending most of the time in a friend's house in St John's Wood, returning to the nursing home only for his daily ray-treatment. Sparrow has offered him some comfortable rooms in All Souls, and he may go there to recuperate.

Last week in London was mercifully quiet, with the evenings dedicated to Oscar. I can quite see how such a task could become an obsession without end. I am *still* deep in *The French Revolution*: the King has just been executed, and I ought to finish on Kisdon, where I have another (pocket) edition. Otherwise my reading is all for Oscar. Tomorrow I must trek out to Putney again to sup with the Ransomes, and on Wednesday I am giving dinner at the Garrick to my bibliographical advisory board, i.e. John Carter, John Hayward and Tim Munby, the Librarian of King's.

The crossword in this week's *Listener* is a teaser, combining ordinary clues, mathematics (which Adam solved in a twinkling) and much information about Norse mythology. What a lot of time you save by not doing them!

6 August 1959   *Grundisburgh*

Mea culpa. I slipped the pen. Not *All's Well* but *Much Ado* was what Routh delighted in at the Gielgud recitation. (Another gaffe! I wrote *As You Like It*!) I had been looking over scores of *As You Like It* scripts; my brain is in a Shakespearean fog. And *en passant* how infinitely I prefer Rosalind to Beatrice—or in fact any other Shakespearean lady. Beatrice no doubt would have been fun to sit next to at dinner, but every day, no thank you. Cleopatra for half the twenty-four hours. Do you remember the lady in the Bülow memoirs who might have married Isvolsky the Russian foreign secretary; after he had reached that eminence, she said, regarding what she had missed: '*Je le regrette tous les jours; je m'en félicite toutes les nuits.*' It is *ad rem* to mention that Isvolsky resembled one of the plainer species of toad (*bufo disgustans*). I read that excellent thing of Gielgud's in *The Times* with great interest. Technique in almost every art and craft always enthrals me. I remember a picture-restorer at Hagley once showing us how he knew a most convincing old picture-frame to be a fake. All forgotten now of course, except that the little worm-holes were so situated that a worm who goes into secret places behind and under the moulding couldn't have made these holes which were all so to say frontal—and were made with tiny shot from an air-pistol. Also wood a hundred and fifty years old brown with age will not—as this did—show white if you take a sliver off the surface with a pen-knife.

How could I possibly be bored with your struggles with Oscar? Surely that must be a best-seller? I shall be taking E. *Marsh* to Cambridge to read in the intervals of deciding whether Pincus and Squance ought to pass and Bytheway and Mange ought to fail. These are actual recent names. One could easily play Cardus's game with them, one eleven, i.e. Beauties—Sunlight, Nice, Bravery, Lettice, Brilliant, Allbless, Mellody, Friendship, Bee, Flowerdew, Divine, v. Beasts—Puddepha, Quass, Jellinek, Sogno, Gutch, Twohig, Bew, Beeny, Beeby, Bobby, and Bones. Tosh and Toh umpires, Mutton and Mimpriss scorers, groundsmen Gasper and Gorbally. Unbelievable but true. The oddest, perhaps of all is apparently quite common in Burmah: it is simply 'Ng'. I should be flummoxed by that at Absence.[1]

I say, how good Ivor is in the new *D.N.B.* on old Agate. I read it in the smallest room in the house this morning—decided in fact that the *D.N.B.* is the perfect lavatory literature. Why does the man Crossman express satisfaction at the gentle debunking, as he calls it, of Henson? Even he and other Wykehamist prigs never wrote a more meaningless sentence. The notice doesn't debunk at all, and why should anyone want H. debunked? He was an excellent bishop, and wrote very much finer English than Crossman ever did or will. How I do hate judgments and prejudices of this kind. And in both *New Statesman* and *Spectator* (a deplorable paper now) the reviews and comments are becoming increasingly cryptic. Are they *all* undergraduates, resolutely showing off? How can Peter F. be happy in that *galère?*

The waggon till September at least? *Very* serious. Did you only just avoid cirrhosis of the liver? You refuse to take it very seriously, but I believe you had a jolly grave illness. Must have been.

Prodger says my wrist is better, and is unmoved by my asking 'Then why does it ache just as much as ever?' His answer is perilously akin to that ancient humbug: 'That shows it is getting better,' but not quite. He is a good man.

The cornfields here look superb, every haulm standing beautifully at attention, so different from last year when every field was as tousled as a third-former's head.

Love to Ruth. I rather think I didn't send it last week, so this is a double lot. So look out, my man.

[1] Eton name for roll-call.

Thunder is rolling round, rain is falling. By the mercy of providence this didn't happen yesterday, when four of us set off at 8.15 a.m. and drove sixty-seven miles to Aldwick, near Bognor, where some old friends have a house on the sea. The sun shone uninterruptedly, and it was so hot that I bathed *four* times. The tide was conveniently high, we took an excellent picnic lunch with us, and the roads (whatever the papers may say) were no worse than any other summer Saturday. Altogether the outing was a thundering success, enjoyed by all. We got back at 8 p.m. Tomorrow morning Duff leaves for Greece, Comfort and Adam go their separate ways on Tuesday, and Ruth and I plan to drive to Kisdon either on Wednesday or (more probably) Thursday. Anyhow write there this week. I can scarcely believe we'll be there so soon. I'm sending this to Cambridge to make sure of its reaching you.

There does not seem to me much chance of Oscar's hitting the best-seller list. It's going to be an enormous book costing several guineas. I hope for extensive reviews, and perhaps translations into foreign languages, but I can't see the common man (whoever he is) rushing out to buy it. Never mind, no doubt pure scholarship is its own reward. I'm still deep in last-minute addenda and corrigenda, but I can see they won't be finished by Wednesday, and the two large cartons of typescript will make their third journey to Kisdon Lodge. I love your lists of candidates' names—clearly much more interesting than the stuff they write. I don't promise to read *How Green* until Oscar has passed out of my control, but we'll see. The *Spectator* has indeed reached rock-bottom, and Fleming has retired to the decent obscurity of an occasional contributor. He drives to Argyllshire tomorrow, ready for the first *battue* on the Twelfth. Once a year they shoot over Kisdon, but most of the grouse are well away from us and we're not bothered.

I had an agreeable dinner last week with my bibliographical friends, but a large jug of the nicest and coldest barley-water doesn't take the place of a glass of wine, and I found myself getting tired and bored before ten. I also journeyed once again to Putney and supped by Arthur Ransome's sickbed. Tomorrow Ruth and I are going to the new Noel Coward play, which I feel may be more amusing than the critics admit: you shall hear.

In bed recently I have re-read *Malice Aforethought* by Francis Iles: it is nearly thirty years old, but I enjoyed it again. Did you ever read it? Otherwise it has been Oscar, Oscar all the way. If this book is nothing else, it will be a mine of information, a sort of *Who's Who* of the Eighties and Nineties in certain circles, social, literary, dramatic etc. I think in your copy I'll have to put an asterisk against the names of all homosexuals in the index (which itself will be hellish long and ever so informative).

(Duff has just rung up to say he's run out of petrol a mile away, and Bridget has driven off with the mowing-machine petrol to his rescue.)

How well do you remember the Marconi scandal? One of my authors is writing a book about it, and I find it most interesting. I was only five when it happened, so missed it as news and have never seen it exhaustively dealt with as history. Rufus Isaacs was, I should say, a pretty slippery customer.

University Arms Hotel
Cambridge

13 August 1959

This really must be a scanty contribution to a correspondence which in quantity, quality and regularity has already reached majestic proportions—because I arrived late last night and your letter which awaited me cannot be dealt with properly till—I suspect—after the post has gone this evening. We shall see.

Cambridge is quite horrible—costive with humanity or at least as Serjeant Buzfuz put it 'beings erect upon two legs and bearing the outward semblance of men and not of monsters'[1] (and the women are worse—damp, bulbous, coffee-coloured). The hotel is grossly over-heated 'because the Americans like it so'. We have just ended the first day's work, in the usual state of complete inability to see *how* we can possibly finish in a week. Did you know that practically all the schools in England begin with B. or C. or W.—and all of them send in several thousand candidates. And of course it becomes clearer every

---

[1] *Pickwick Papers*, chapter xxxiv.

year that *examination* on set English books is absurd, meaningless, and demoralising to all concerned—the cheque that comes at the end is the only sound and sensible thing about it.

I have brought a Trollope to read in the intervals, viz *Can You Forgive Her?* What fantastic titles he did light on. But *how* good they are—*real* people and you really want to know what is going to happen to them. *Miles* better than AUSTEN (Hush!)

Did you see my letter in Saturday's *Daily Telegraph*? Very odd. Everyone I ask says they read the *D.T.* Not one saw the letter. It was merely a little tale about an old Lord Chief Justice which hit a certain nail on the head. Perhaps nobody ever reads the correspondence column. It is usually full of rubbish.

Malice Aforethought I remember thinking awfully good, but I never can remember who F. Iles really is. I like your plan about 'my' Oscar (bless you) with the starred homos: it will look like Baedeker.

In re Marconi, look up the poem by Kipling beginning 'Well done Gehazi', addressed to Rufus Isaacs. It was a sorry show, full of stout lying.

16 August 1959   *Kisdon Lodge*

Our dear farmer is not at the moment milking up here, so we no longer have our milk and post brought up for us, but yesterday we went down to shop at Hawes, and there was your letter waiting at Keld post office—which is also the local Youth Hostel, kept by an admirable Yorkshireman and his wife. He comes from Keighley, but despises his fellow West Riding men as busybodies and much prefers the people here. He is great friends with our farmer, who lives next door to him.

You seem a little harassed in your letter, and I only hope that strong doses of Trollope taken at bedtime will preserve your health and sanity. T's titles are excellent, but so were others of the time. I particularly like *What will he Do with it?* and *Red as a Rose is She*. To my mind these are almost as good as *Have With You to Saffron Walden*,[1] surely the best ever.

[1] By Bulwer Lytton; Rhoda Broughton; Thomas Nashe.

Alas, I never see the *Daily Telegraph* unless it is sent in mistake for . *The Times*. Have you a copy of your letter? I would return it faithfully.

You seem to have been much less surprised at the B.B.C. Advisory Council[1] than I was. Anyhow I shall look forward to discussing grey-hound racing with the Bishop of Manchester, and the steel industry with Gubby Allen—and you shall hear all about it.

I think it was Maurice Baring (but you will correct me) who said he had decided that the *Iliad* and the *Odyssey* weren't written by Homer, but by another man of the same name. The saying, *pari passu*, goes for Francis Iles, whose real name is A.B. Cox.

Today has been pure joy: brilliant sunshine and a deep blue sky with the whitest cotton-wool clouds flying over the mountains. We had breakfast, lunch and tea outside and didn't speak to anyone else all day. I think I told you that when we first came here we discovered, deep under the turf which came right up to the cottage door, a fine set of huge flagstones forming a little terrace in front, and on either side a path to coalshed and E.C. Well, today we found a lot more, buried even deeper, which complete and enlarge the path to the coal-shed. We had tremendous fun digging them out in the sunshine, and I can see that the rearrangement and levelling of them will take us ages. If we have another hot day we plan to drive about sixty miles to a place called Saltburn-by-the-Sea, which we once briefly visited and liked enormously. It is a small, entirely Victorian seaside place, de-signed for the toiling millions of Stockton and Middlesbrough. It is south of Redcar and north of Whitby. It has sands and a little pier, and there is a thin black line of coal-dust at the edge of the water. The drive to it is all countrified.

Having been up here only six weeks ago, we dropped back quicker than ever into the delicious rhythm of the place, and our only com-plaint is that the hours fly past too quickly. Oscar still claims every possible moment, and even as I write this Ruth is looking through our vast typescript for this and that. Finding one letter or reference may take hours. Outside in the sun today I read all through the 600-page bibliography of O's writings, and found a mass of tiny things I had missed earlier. Clearly one could go on like this for ever, but I *must*

[1] Of which I had just been made a temporary member.

reach some sort of conclusion by the end of this month, or the publishing business will wither.

At night I am *still* Carlyle-ing, and have now passed Charlotte Corday. Ruth is reading Henry James by day and a detective story in the evenings. We had sausages, fried potatoes and beans for lunch, followed by apple pie and stewed blackberries. An occasional grouse, hare or curlew passes by: there is a water shortage in all the Dale villages, but our spring trickles on, and all the fields are incredibly *green*. The brown tops of the fells are now purple with heather. All the hill-farmers are so used to taking three months to get their hay in, because the weather is never right, that this year, when every field was harvested by mid-July, they don't know what to do with themselves in August: a few days' beating for the local shoots perhaps.

Did I tell you that Ruth's son is going to be married to a charming American girl in October? Anyhow the young couple are coming up here next week-end to spend a day with us. We are meeting them at Richmond (thirty miles) and have got them rooms at an inn about halfway from there. Although it's an intolerable nuisance having *anyone* here, they're both delightful, and their arrival will give us an opportunity to clean and tidy everything, so as to show off the cottage at its best. We pray for a fine clear day like to-day—when one could see into Westmorland, and almost watch Roger making impish comments at his desk—but I expect they'll get a drizzling day with no visibility.

Alas, there seem to be no sales while we're here. Since the local paper didn't appear for seven weeks, I daresay many sales were postponed and will now take place just too late for us.

Ruth says she much enjoys the affectionate messages you send her —and would send a lot back if only the censor would pass them.

21 August 1959   *Grundisburgh*

It hasn't happened often before, but I am afraid this letter won't arrive till Monday. Your letter was not coughed up by the hotel until Wednesday evening, and we had a great rush all that day and Thursday, which left us all rather limp. You never can tell in this awarding;

if you run up against a mad examiner you may spend three hours on work which should take one. On Wednesday a man (ex-don) turned up who quite often gave eight to an answer that was worth sixteen. He evidently was marking fifteen–sixteen-year-olds on a Tripos standard. Curses both loud *and* deep accompanied the re-readership of his scripts. But all is over now and we are home again—Pamela from Holland which she much enjoyed. The Lawrences were in their caravan and she nearby in a sort of Dutch council-house—far cleaner than an English ditto would be, though quite primitive. Another thing which struck her was the enormous amount the Dutch eat; her landlady was convinced that P. must surely starve to death after seeing what an infinitesimal portion she ate of the six thick slices of bread, the two eggs, ham, cheese (!) etc which they put on the breakfast-table.

Your address. Do you suppose that though away from home I have not got it in my pocket? And now in fact it is pretty secure in my head, though that may become a blank at any moment. *Can You Forgive Her?* just lasted out the bed-time reading night and morning. A rum lot the Vavasors—and that old stick Planty Pal; and one could make a lot of adverse comments, but how *readable* it all is. How little many people have read, whose job one would have thought needed a good deal more—e.g. an English Lit. examiner of fifty or so, who was reading *Howards End*, 'the first one of Forster's I have ever read'. He teaches Eng. Lit. too, at some not wholly dim school. That would not happen in Germany surely? And my colleagues, who know all about John Osborne, Lawrence etc., had never even heard of Father Damien and the Stevenson letter. And one of them foams at the mouth at the memory of having once been asked to read Carlyle's *Life of John Sterling*—on the odd grounds that he hates Carlyle's 'Teutonism', of which there is no more in *J.S.* than there is any of Kipling's jingoism in *The Jungle Books*. Fancy any Eng. Lit. teacher not knowing Carlyle's description of Coleridge at Highgate!

Do you include in your good titles *Is He Popenjoy?*[1] which I can't quite swallow, though I seem to remember it as excellent reading. I remember little nowadays of anything recently read.

[1] By Anthony Trollope.

I was stupidly thinking 'Well done, Gehazi' was the first line of the poem. No, here it is in R.K.'s collected poems simply called 'Gehazi' (1915). It is pretty blistering, but I suppose Rufus Isaacs blandly ignored it. Has A.B. Cox ever written under his own name, or any other but *Malice Aforethought* under F. Iles? It was very good. Don't I remember a masterly first sentence, something like: 'It was during the Vicarage Garden party that X decided to murder his wife'? Tell me, by the way, about Simenon. They all say he is so good, but I must have struck some of his offday stories, e.g. *Maigret in Montmartre* which I read on yesterday's journey. It seemed to me well enough, but not more, and Maigret himself showed no particular genius. What would you recommend of Simenon's?

I met Bob Boothby at Cambridge and liked him; he was excellent company and very friendly. What good stories they tell of old Beecham the conductor. I like his 'What an artist!' when a donkey brought into some opera rehearsal brayed, followed by 'And what a critic!' when it copiously evacuated on the stage. No doubt you knew it.

I once went to Saltburn, though I cannot remember when or why. I don't recollect the coaldust at the water's edge. In your letter you make it sound like an additional attraction. I like to hear that Ruth keeps two books going at once, because I always do (I *have* had three). Tell me of any really good recent Penguins. Otherwise I shall really have to re-read in bed W.W. Jacobs, *Earlham* and *The Irish R.M.*—not that there are not worse fates than that (my Cambridge colleagues, by the way, think nothing of the last, but I suspect they haven't read it— in the Quiller-Couch sense of 'reading').

My letter in the *D.T.* I merely, via an old hero, hit a full pitch to leg. Some ass had suggested that the Tories after nine years are tired and 'voters should give the others a run'. I recalled the old Lord Chief Justice who, his friends hinted, should retire, one reason being that he often went to sleep on the Bench. He grunted and then asked who would succeed him. When they said 'X', he snorted and said: 'Well, let me tell you, I do much less harm asleep that X would do awake.'

Love to Ruth. Good news about her son. One knows such sad tales of a mother finding her son's choice of a wife wholly wrong.

You were quite right, and your excellent letter reached me only this morning. In fact this suited well, since our week-end was much occupied with the visit of Ruth's son and his intended. On Saturday (the last day of a week of superb sunshine) we drove to meet them at Richmond (which is *not* thirty miles away, as I told you last week, but only twenty-three), picnicked with them on the moors and brought them back here. Yesterday they came back for lunch, after which we drove them back to Richmond. By then the weather had broken, and the mountain-tops (including ours) were blanketed in damp clouds. Today a gale is raging, and by ill luck this is the evening on which we arranged to climb down the hill and sup with our benevolent farmer and his family. So I may not be able to post this till tomorrow.

As usual, we have decided to steal an extra day here, and will now drive south on Thursday. The next day (Friday) is my fifty-second birthday, and Ruth is planning a little dinner-party in her Hampstead house, at which Comfort (who returns from France that day) will be present. On Saturday morning C. and I will go down to Bromsden, where I shall hope to find your letter waiting.

Gradually, in the evenings and at odd moments, we are filling up the lacunae in the Oscar notes, and I am re-writing the worst of them. Ruth is now reading the whole damned thing through, with the notes, to make sure they are in the right places etc.

A.B. Cox has, so far as I know, never published anything under his own name, but many years ago he wrote a number of quite good detective stories as Anthony Berkeley (which I suppose are his Christian names). As Francis Iles he published one other suspense-story, called *Before the Fact*. I haven't set eyes on a copy for ages, but remember thinking it good, if a trifle inferior to *Malice A*. Simenon is excellent at his best, but he has written so much that, although I've read most of them, I can't now remember which is which. You may well have struck an inferior one. I should try some more—perhaps non-Maigret ones, for M. is, as you say, not wildly exciting. Simenon's greatest gift is that of conjuring up the feel and atmosphere of French seaports and small towns in the minimum of words and almost without adjectives. Maupassant had this gift, but S. is even more successful at it. My favourite Beecham story is of the instrumentalist who played a wrong note at rehearsal. Beecham tapped for silence and then asked: 'What's your name?' 'Ball, Sir Thomas', said the culprit. 'H'm,' said Beecham, 'singular!' Cardus, a great friend and admirer of B's, has a fund of good stories about him. And now I see he has married another young girl—well, well!

(Now I must change and descend the mountain. More anon.)

10.45 p.m. We have just staggered up the hill, blown out by endless home-made cakes etc. Luckily we borrowed a powerful flashlight from our hosts, for the night is pitch-black, with a gale blowing.

Last Monday we duly drove to Saltburn (sixty-two miles, all country) and spent a happy day on the beach. I bathed three times, R. once. The rest of the week we simply basked outside the cottage, all meals alfresco, and we are both sunburnt as though by Riviera sun. At long last I have finished *The French Revolution*, and I somehow doubt whether, for all its splendid flashes, I shall ever read it again. When I get home I shall start on *Past and Present*: searching for Oscar's quotations is certainly enlarging my scope, and I don't need much excuse to launch out into well-worn but by-me-neglected paths.

I imagine you are likely to be invaded by grandchildren for the next few weeks, and can see you sheltering from them in your summer-house. Alas, we haven't taken any more snapshots for your delectation: hot sunshine begets a delicious lethargy in which reading *The Times* is a hard day's work—even yesterday's *Times*. And often we don't breakfast till 10. Lingering over breakfast is the office-worker's first step to liberation. Do you remember Birrell's remark: 'Chippendale, the cabinet-maker, is more potent than Garrick, the actor. The vivacity of the latter no longer charms (save in Boswell); the chairs of the former still render rest impossible in a hundred homes.' I copy it out irrelevantly because I have just come across it quoted by Oscar and enjoyed it. Now it is time to light our candles and go up to bed. The wind is raging outside: otherwise there is no sound save the quiet tick of the grandfather clock. This is the place for us.

Ruth insists on sending her love.

Good! The old rhythm is re-established—systole and diastole don't they call it? I don't know exactly what they/it mean(s), and strongly sympathise with the embryo science-student who wrote that in all human affairs could be observed a regular movement of sisterly and disasterly. How G.K.C. would have loved that and brilliantly demonstrated the profound truth of the remark—just as he did of the apparently faulty definition that an optimist was a man who looked after one's eyes and the pessimist one's feet.

I am in the summer-house—after a month during which it was far too hot. And of course this would be the day on which Pamela is turning me out of it and entertaining; and all the afternoon and evening the garden will be full of shapeless old women, led by a vivacious nonagenarian named Mrs Shadrach Gray. She used to darn my socks and when I questioned her charge of one penny per sock as being absurdly small, she replied firmly that it was what she charged in 1897 and why should she change?

Odd about your gale. Suffolk has known nothing but sunshine and calm for weeks, and my frame of mind approaches that of Keats's bees[1] —and *my* cells have been pretty clammy of late. At anything over 78° I am like the psalmist, poured out like water. Marking papers has really been as good an occupation as anything more active. I have not quite finished yet—nothing from British Guiana having turned up, and I await without enthusiasm about 180 lucubrations on *Great Expectations*. And I want to hear no more about Joe Gargery or Magwitch as long as I live.

That is most interesting about A.B. Cox, because I always read any Anthony Berkeley I could get hold of. I wonder why he is so anonymous? And weren't you impressed by my remembering the first sentence of *M.A.*? I haven't seen it for twenty-five years. I had it, but some brute of a boy pinched it. I will try some more Simenon but you don't raise my hopes very high. Maigret is an imposter. Lestrade and even Athelney Jones[1] would have thought nothing of his work in the Montmartre book. His atmosphere I agree is good. Thank you for the

[1] In his 'Ode to Autumn'.

Beecham quip—very typical. Send me any more you come across. None so far reported is below first-class, unlike many in the Eddie Marsh book in which I am at the moment submerged. Not at all bored, though it really is too long, and the beer at times is very small. I find myself beginning to like E.M. You knew him no doubt—and will be able to tell me why he was always spoken of with more or less genial mockery. Was it the combination of eyeglass and voice and eyebrows or what? He had a far better head and heart than most of those who sneered at him.

Of course you won't read *The French Revolution* again—but you will sometimes dip into it in search of some half-remembered gem of phraseology or characterisation. What a vivid power the 'thrawn old peasant' had. Do you know his life? I never read the immense one (Wilson), but once knew Froude pretty well. The best short one I know is Garnett's—not in the English Men of Letters. You will like the past part of *Past and Present* and put Abbot Samson among your heroes. I never much took to Jane C. (nor did Browning!) and find her famous letters over-praised. Recently I was pleased to be told (by whom?) that she traded on her repute as a raconteur and could be very long-winded and boring. Wasn't that Geraldine Jewsbury association all rather dubious?

Talking of length, the Ipswich library, pursuing its policy of acquiring the most expensive and least readable literature, has just got three obese volumes of Theodore Dreiser's letters. I browsed on them for half-an-hour yesterday with very little pleasure or profit. A dullish dog surely? He wrote in 1941 that he would prefer to see the Germans established in England rather than the continuance in power of aristocratic fox-hunters. In brief he was pontificating without sense or point. Some friend at his English publishers protested and D. replied, addressing him more than once as 'darling', sticking to his views but hoping for no loss of friendship. I was pleased to see no further letter from or to this good man.

The garden swarms with offspring and I contemplate them as Macbeth did the descendants of Banquo, though considerably less

---

¹ 'When Gregson, or Lestrade, or Athelney Jones are out of their depths—which, by the way, is their normal state—the matter is laid before me,' said Sherlock Holmes (*The Sign of Four*, chapter one).

horrified.[1] Pamela of course is in her element, ceaselessly busy, and obviously enjoying every moment.

P.S. Millions of good wishes for your birthday. Let me tell you fifty-two is just about the prime of life in many more ways than not. Of course if you still want to high-jump or waltz all night it isn't, but for calm enjoyment of the passing show, for freedom of taste, and indifference to fashion, it is the right age.

Love to Ruth. I have carried myself several inches taller since she 'insisted' on sending her love!

30 *August 1959*   *Bromsden Farm*

Your letter was faithfully awaiting me yesterday, on top of a fortnight's worth of bills, newspapers and circulars. Systole and diastole were repeatedly used by Carlyle to describe the action of the guillotine, so I suppose it will do to describe the ebb and flow of our correspondence—ah well, the tide's out here, as the talkative lady in *Juno and the Paycock* declared, holding out her empty glass.

Leaving Kisdon was agony, as ever. Our last day was gloriously hot and sunny, as was the day of departure. We locked the door of the cottage (after stopping the grandfather clock) at 10.30, ate our lunch and tea by the wayside, took it fairly easy, and reached Soho Square at 9.30 p.m. Friday was a mass of visitors, correspondence and other nonsense. Ruth's birthday dinner in Hampstead had to be postponed till 10 p.m., when Comfort belatedly arrived from France. The noise of London once again seemed intolerable, its air foetid, after the silent freshness of Kisdon, and next June seems a very long way off. I was indeed impressed by your memory of *Malice Aforethought's* opening, and would have been even more so if you had got it right! The immortal sentence runs: 'It was not until several weeks after he had decided to murder his wife that Dr Bickleigh took any active steps in the matter.'

[1] 'What, will the line stretch out to the crack of doom?' (*Macbeth*, act iv, scene i).

I can't at the moment remember any more Beecham quips, but I recall Cardus describing how B. once rang him up from Leeds (or somewhere even more distant) and discoursed for half an hour, apropos of nothing, on English music from Purcell to Delius. Knowing B's dislike of Elgar, Cardus at last interjected 'What about Elgar?' To which Beecham: 'What about him? Is he ill?'

Your reaction to the Eddie Marsh book was exactly mine, but I read it on Kisdon in paradise, where critical judgment is blunted by joy. I knew Eddie for many years, and it was impossible not to laugh at his squeaky voice, extraordinary gestures and general twitter.

I began *Past and Present* last night in bed, but sleep overcame me after two chapters. I've got the huge Wilson biography, but it's in fact a gigantic source-book rather than a biography. Froude is excellent, though now factually suspect in places. I'm sure Mrs Carlyle must have been hell, but the old boy can't have been too easy to live with. Have you ever visited their house in Chelsea? It's a museum containing all their furniture and many relics—austere, uncomfortable and very interesting. The nicest great-man's-house I've seen was Napoleon's Malmaison, where the library is a gem.

Theodore Dreiser's books are enough to stop me in my tracks, never mind his letters—that slovenly turgid style describing endless business deals, with a seduction every hundred pages as light relief. If he's the great American novelist, give me the Marx Brothers every time.

I loved your description of my age as the prime of life, and only wish I had more time for 'the calm enjoyment of the passing show.' Next week is already hideous with engagements, and I can see the doors of the prison house inexorably closing. Chaos still follows the printing strike, and we shall have to put off ten books to 1960. In a way this is a good thing, since it will obscure what would otherwise have been the hiatus caused by my three-months absence and the non-acceptance of any books (if you see what I mean) during that time. I usually publish just under fifty books a year—almost one a week, so we would normally be twelve short for next year. I'm not sure whether *The Lion* has gone to you yet: if not it shall go next week, when fresh supplies are promised.

Peter looked in this afternoon. While he was shooting in Scotland he was attacked by pleurisy, refused to pay any attention, went on shooting, and seems none the worse. He is an extraordinary chap.

At the birthday dinner on Friday I had my first glass of wine since April, didn't enjoy it much and felt no better for it, so I think I shall continue my teetotalism a little longer.

The garden here is unusually ablaze with flowers, particularly zinnias, which love the sun. Most of the grass is parched, and Comfort is having great trouble in transplanting seedling wallflowers. To-morrow Ruth and I are going to *The Aspern Papers*, on which I will report next week.

I had a feeble hope that membership of that ridiculous B.B.C. committee would include a new radio set, but it seems they only run to free copies of the *Listener* and *Radio Times*. I can't wait for the first meeting.

2 September 1959   *Grundisburgh*

Well!! I could have almost *sworn* in a law-court that at least there was something about a garden-party in the first sentence of *Malice Aforethought*. And I have no copy, and it is out of print. Why isn't it in the Penguins? There are very many worse. I grant you it is not *very* impressive to remember a thing wrong. The number of things I am certain about diminishes rapidly; the day no doubt approaches when I shall have forgotten who played for England at Edgbaston in 1902—the side that Plum thinks the strongest that ever did. And we lost the rubber!

I have finished *Eddie Marsh*, and it is my considered opinion (as the specialist said in the advertisements of Lamplough's Pyretic Saline) that it would be hard to mention half-a-dozen people who did more good (using the word in Aristotle's sense, viz from a good motive, in a good way, and with good results) in a lifetime than he did. Your word 'twitter' holds the reason of his absurdity. About many (most?) of his written judgments there is no twitter at all. The way he stuck to his opinions, generally *very* sound ones, is admirable. As to voice, it is odd to remember that Bismarck, of all people, had a thin falsettoish voice.

It should have been that of Stentor, or at least Frank Harris. There is not much sign of Winston or Somerset Maugham laughing at E.M.

Yes, poor old Carlyle, as his mother said, was 'gey ill to deal wi' ', which Froude, in his loose way, often writes as 'to *live* with', which is very different. I have twice been over the Carlyle House, as well as the one at Ecclefechan (*not* Craigenputtock!), as you say an ugly uncomfortable house, with its absurd sound-proof room on the top floor, which was a complete failure, as anyone could have told him it would be if the ceiling wasn't doubled like the walls. They didn't know much about dyspepsia then (do they now?) but surely some doctor ought to have stopped him having what he calls an 'innocent spoonful of porridge' just before going to bed. Did you ever hear of a stranger 'nightcap'?

I am trying to set a paper on *Julius Caesar* in which no question is repeated that was set in any of the *four* papers in the last five or six years. And it is really not possible, as whoever thinks there are more than sixteen questions that can be asked on the play is like the cricket enthusiast who claimed that Trumper had seven different ways of dealing with a yorker. I think I shall try a quotation from old Agate, viz that Brutus is 'a magnanimous ass,' but it won't pass the revisers —I tried it on before. J.A.'s calling Richard II 'a muff' was objected to on the grounds that many candidates would not know what a muff was. It is true that the number of candidates who don't understand plain English steadily increases. 'Reading' was once set as one of the essay subjects, and produced several answers all about biscuits.

Sorry about your getting only the *Listener* and *Radio Times* for your good counsel on the B.B.C. committee. The former is as often as not unreadable. *Punch* is completely so. I understand hardly a thing in it. Does anybody read it? And who is the new editor of the *T.L.S.*? Pryce-Jones passed out of it very quietly.

Apart from professional football, is there anything more boring than everything about an election except the actual results? Roger's fatuous [Liberal] party is going to dish a good many Tory marginal M.P.s. I wish I had the smallest belief in democracy in action as opposed to in theory, in which of course we all believe. Old Inge in his *Evening Standard* articles had a nice right and left, one from Creighton: 'Socialism won't work till all men are perfect, and then it won't be needed', and 'A Labor program is one which leaves out "u" and "me"'. We live in the constituency of Eye, and our member is much the stupidest man in the country. Who is your member? I should be quite prepared to hear that you don't know, holding with the Doctor the sound if rather cacophonous view: 'How small, of all that human hearts endure, That part which laws or kings can cause or cure'.[1]

6 September 1959   *Bromsden Farm*

There *is* a garden party at the beginning of *Malice Aforethought*, so you weren't so far wrong. The trouble about Eddie Marsh was that, despite all the goodness you so rightly praise, he seemed (and in many ways *was*) exceedingly *silly*. For instance, his handling of Mrs Brooke (impossible old bitch though she was) was maladroit in the extreme. H.G. Wells and Arnold Bennett both had squeaky voices, but they weren't silly: perhaps impotence has its own brand of silliness.

The unreadable *Punch* has asked me to be drawn for 'a posy of publishers' which they are planning. I have graciously consented, so look out! The new *T.L.S.* editor is a charming chap called Arthur Crook, who has long been doing all the work there.

I propose to take as little notice as possible of the General Election. Henley is a safe Conservative seat, and the sitting member, John Hay, has some minor ministerial job. They say he's pretty good, but how do I know?

Last Tuesday my old father (age 81) drove to the Grand Hotel, Eastbourne, for a fortnight's holiday. He was accompanied by a twenty-four-year-old waitress called Iris, posing as his niece. Until recently he took such about with him for dalliance, but now it's simply, I fancy, for companionship, though how a cultivated man can long endure the conversation of an illiterate Cockney girl is rather baffling. Anyhow, the very first night the old boy fell over in the bathroom and (it appears) pulled a muscle, or something of the sort. He spent the next three days in bed in the hotel, and on Friday I heard that he was being moved to a nursing home. Iris then left for home, and as my sister is

---

[1] Dr Johnson, 'Lines added to Goldsmith's *Traveller*'.

away in Scotland I thought I ought to visit the old fellow. So yester-day morning I left here at 9.15 in our old Morris station-waggon and drove the hundred miles to Eastbourne. The roads were crammed with sea-going traffic, and the journey took me three and a half hours. Several times I thought I must be behind a funeral, and eventually I found I was! It was a glorious day, and the countryside (all crops harvested) looked benignly autumnal—plenty of mellow fruitfulness, and thank God no mists. I hit the sea-front at 12.45, immediately plunged into the sea (which I always adore), and then sat on the beach for a couple of hours, eating the excellent lunch Comfort had given me and reading a book about Oscar—very enjoyable. Then I visited my father. The nursing home is a Catholic one, run by Irish nuns, and since he is a violent Agnostic I was amused to find him sur-rounded by holy pictures and statues of the Virgin. I took him some flowers and books, and was reassured by his comparative comfort and the bottles of whisky with which he had come armed. I stayed an hour with him, ate an excellent tea, and drove home. There was so much less traffic that the return journey took three quarters of an hour less than the outward one, and I was home by seven, slightly tired but ever so virtuous. All of which puts me further back in my manuscript-reading etc.

Last Monday Ruth and I took our American friends to *The Aspern Papers*, which is first-rate—continuously dramatic and perfectly acted. I know you never go to the theatre, but I know you'd like this if you could hear it. On Tuesday I trekked out to Putney, and was delighted to find old Ransome much improved. He was able to get out of bed and totter with two sticks into the dining-room. His wife is thinking of taking him to Brighton for a change: he has been in bed since Christmas, and I was beginning to fear he would never rise again.

One day I lunched at the Ritz Grill, one with some rich City merchant-bankers, one with the wife of a millionaire—all for business reasons—so you can see that I am rapidly being dragged back into the whirlpool. London is full of visiting Americans and Canadians, who take up a lot of time, and I can't tell you how I long for the peace of Swaledale and my one perfect companion.

Donald Somervell is out of the nursing home, but he doesn't sound at all well. I'm going to see him tomorrow.

Oscar *still* hasn't gone to the printer, but it's no good trying to be a perfectionist if one hasn't got the time.

Well anyway there *was* a garden-party. But I am still slightly put about at having misquoted so badly, rather (to compare small things with great) like the great scholar Ingram Bywater when someone reading a commentator's note came across the Latin word '*scillicus*'. I.B. lugged down a dictionary (I quote R.W. Chapman) and read out '*scillicus*: It means the forty-eighth part of an *as*, and, by metonymy, a comma'. Then replacing the book, and turning to his audience, in accents of unfeigned dismay—'I didn't *know* that!' But the memory in old age! I remember the shock when C.M. Wells a few years ago re-called how Percy Lubbock and Alec Cadogan sat next to each other in Sixth Form. But Alas! A.C. came to Benson's a half or two before P.L. left. And C.M.W. had the Cambridge trait (defect?) of never making a statement unless he was sure of its truth.

Talking of misquotations, I hope you saw that my admirable nephew[1] after visiting Stevenson's grave in Samoa offered £50 to have the misquote 'home from *the* sea' put right on his headstone? I call that a good gesture, but I have no doubt that one of the sillier socialists, like that ass among the apostles, will grumble that it wasn't put into the poor-box.

E. Marsh. Yes, I see. That silliness. I suppose Winston and Maugham were cute enough to see through it. He certainly sounded rather silly when I met him at Roger's. But he was very old then, and spent most of the evening to, from, and in the water-closet, his bladder having clearly thrown up the sponge, literally and metaphorically. I wonder if Mrs Brooke was manageable at all. Perhaps we enter there that dim cave of physiological spleen, breezily referred to by a medical friend of mine who stated that—as he put it—'*all* women instinctively dislike a eunuch'. Do you know anything of this? Surely it must have been the theme of many manuscripts offered to you.

[1] Charles John Lyttelton, tenth Viscount Cobham (1909–1977), Captain of Worcestershire cricket side 1936–1939, Governor-General of New Zealand 1957–1962.

I am interested to hear what you say about the modern treatment of jaundice. New since my day (nine years ago). I don't expect it has reached Suffolk yet. My own doctor is a charming man, but knows very little. I hope you will be back in the convivial world at the October Lit. Soc.

How good you are about visiting invalids! Tell me about D. Somervell. He is a bright spot at the Lit. Soc. And your bankers and millionaires. Are these last ever happy? A few days ago the *Daily Telegraph* had a picture of the richest man in the world—capital £700m. A face with *no* expression except gloom, worry, and dyspepsia. Bankrupts *per contra* invariably look plump, hilarious, and obviously without a care in the world. It is a solemn thought that on Wednesday you are about two million pounds richer than you were on the previous Wednesday. Isn't Nuffield about the only *actively* benevolent millionaire we know of? What a reflection on those Mellons etc. Perhaps, like Bernard Shaw they are all convinced in their old age that they are ruined.

13 September 1959   *Bromsden Farm*

Thank goodness *The Lion* has reached you at last: I only hope it doesn't disappoint you. Adlai Stevenson should be on its heels, 'but with unhurrying chase and unperturbed pace'—forgive me; I have just agreed to open the Francis Thompson centenary exhibition at Preston on October 29, and am brushing up my memory of that remarkable poem,[1] parts of which (as much as you would let me) I once recited to you so as to escape Early School. Luckily I still think *very* highly of F.T., so should be able to fill thirty unforgiving minutes of jaw about him.

I missed the news of your nephew's splendidly quixotic offer about the misprint on Stevenson's tomb, but what a fine gesture!

You simply mustn't start worrying about the General Election, which, except for casting my vote before swine, I propose to ignore. Did you see the (I think Giles) cartoon of the man, promised daily election talks, junking off his television set to the rag-and-bone man?

[1] 'The Hound of Heaven'.

The possibility of switching the machine off is seldom mentioned, but then I've never had a set and am ignorant of its seductive power. As for Mrs Brooke, Eddie, and the proposition that all women instinctively dislike a eunuch, alas, I lack experience to answer you, but it seems quite likely.

If you haven't read *The Aspern Papers*, you must do so at once: it's one of H.J.'s best. None of his own plays had any success at all—and rightly, for they were no good. His stories are packed with drama (now being exploited by others), but he lacked the one essential dramatist's gift—an instinctive sense of exactly what will *go* in the theatre.

I visited Donald Somervell again last week—in a friend's house in a noisy part of St John's Wood, miles beyond Lord's. He was up and dressed, and we sat out on a flower-filled balcony, but he looked terribly thin and pale, and his whole state sadly reminded me of another friend who died of much the same thing (a growth on the bladder) some months after undergoing the agonising deep-ray treatment which Donald has just endured. However, I pray the cases may be quite different, and he was cheerful enough, though when I left, his lady protector said he hadn't laughed like that for weeks. I shall try and go again.

I've no idea whether bankers and millionaires are ever happy, but my luncheon hostess told me that Mr Clore takes as much trouble about buying a picture for £20,000 (£4. 10. 0 to you or me) as in acquiring a business for several millions. Sounds kinda dreary to me. But the Mellons have given away countless millions in the U.S.A. The National Gallery itself, in Washington, was financed by them.

I'm ashamed to tell you that Oscar *still* hasn't gone to the printer: more and more letters and facts keep cropping up, and it seems silly to run up unnecessary bills for proof-corrections if I can do them now. And I have very little time. The other day Shane Leslie told me that one of Oscar's boys was caricatured in Michael Arlen's *The Green Hat*, so I re-read it (the first time since it appeared when I was at Eton) and was astonished to find how readable and interesting it was. The plot is ridiculous and much of the dialogue fantastic, but the book has a definite quality beyond the curiosity of a period piece. I remember in 1930 asking Somerset Maugham what he thought of Arlen's books, and he said 'The first thing to remember is that he's an Armenian, an Oriental'. I now see that he was right: this book is like something by the author of *The Arabian Nights* set down in London and Paris of the 1920s. I hesitate to suggest your reading, or re-reading, the book, and simply report its unexpected effect on me. Into what unexpected places do the rigours of research carry one! (Incidentally Shane Leslie was right, and I got the reference for my note.) At the same time I'm plodding through *Past and Present*, and so far plodding is the *mot juste*, but I suspect there is better to come. I've got more than a dozen books out of the London Library, all containing Oscar references which I haven't yet had time to consider. The job, I fear, is endless.

Here the garden is Sahara-dry and even the sun-loving zinnias hang their heads till the reviving hose is brought their way. Adam shoots the squirrels as they come for the walnuts, which aren't any good anyhow. All our apples are dropping off, but I revel in the sunshine and dread the end of summer-time. Peter can't wait for October and the pheasant's death-knell. They are taking up most of Soho Square with a pneumatic drill.

16 September 1959   *Grundisburgh*

I had forgotten that your Early School exemption choice was the Hound. A very good one too. And you have never forgotten it—which of course was my *raison d'être*. Luckily the authorities never found out, or I should have been scuppered. They would have asked for a ruling, and of course the whole arrangement was *ultra vires*. I never did any action of the entire rightness of which I am more certain. I should like to hear your jaw. Will it be taken down? If so—!

I shall tell my nephew of your reaction, which will please him immensely. It certainly ought to be widely known that one Governor-General has a right sense of values.

How right you are about the election. I wish I could be as philosophical, but I am like Ovid, '*Video meliora proboque, Deteriora sequor*'[1] (he was writing of morals!). There was a very good article by Hollis in the *Spectator* in which he pointed out that the scurrilities used to be

[1] I see and approve better things, but follow worse (*metamorphoses*, vii, 20).

confined to *hoi polloi*, while the leaders of the parties thundered high-mindedly in the upper air, but TV etc has changed all that; leaders have to talk to the Eatanswill voters in the voters' own language. *Hinc illae lacrimae.* It is an odd thought that Mr Gladstone could and did address a working-class audience for one and a quarter hours in the open air on the subject of the disestablishment of the Irish Church —and held their attention. Can the present bigwigs do that? No. They carry no ice, as Jimmy Thomas said to Eddie Marsh, who corroborated it by adding 'and cut no guns'.

I note what you say of *The Aspern Papers*. I suppose if poor old H.J. had collaborated with Pinero or Sardou his plays might have run. I doubt if I ever read the book. What a persistent posthumous success the old boy is having.

I withdraw *in toto* my smear about the Mellons. I had no idea old Andrew had been such a patron of the arts. Must have confused him with someone else.

You will not, I hope, omit to drink to the immortal memory on Friday. Half the papers seem to think the Doctor was born on the 13th. Why? Have we monkeyed with the calendar since his day? And has the dinner taken place, with old Powell as cheer-leader? We ought to get some American fan to endow the club handsomely, so that it could really provide a good dinner in the famous room, and not among the spittoons and cigarette-ends of the Cheshire Cheese. But such nice things don't happen.

20 September 1959   *Bromsden Farm*

I sincerely hope that my Francis Thompson 'jaw' will not be taken down—even for your edification. In about three weeks' time I shall bitterly regret having accepted their invitation, and thank goodness I had the wit the other day to decline to address two hundred French schoolmasters in London, welcoming them to London in an *hour's* talk! The French Embassy offered to pay my 'usual fee', but a joke's a joke.

I'm all for harnessing the sea, but I should hate its salt to be removed, since it must be that very salt I so much enjoy in sea-bathing.

I care little for swimming in rivers, and abominate swimming-baths. Give me 'the unplumb'd, *salt*, estranging sea.'[1]

If I had any money I should take every possible step to make sure the Government didn't get it at my death. A close friend of Comfort's married (as his second wife) a charming old boy who was old enough to be her father. He was clearly wealthy and they lived in style, but she never liked to ask him about money. When he died (in his eighties) he left £400,000, of which the Government took £300,000. She was wild with rage and couldn't understand why he hadn't given their two children large presents. Nor can I.

Adam went back to Eton on Wednesday, and yesterday I drove over to take the three things he had forgotten—his portable wireless, his *braces* and the funds (some £3 in a small tobacco tin) of the Eton College Chess Club, of which he is (however unsuitably) treasurer.

Last week I again journeyed to Putney to sup with the Ransomes, but he is so much better that they are going to his sister's in the country for a change, so I shan't have to visit them for a few weeks.

I had a note from Donald S. to say he has gone to his brother's in Kent, so my visiting list is mercifully reduced. My old father is back in London, so I suppose I shall have to look in on him one day.

Peter is flying north tonight for three more days of grouse-shooting. Shooting is like a religion to him—something solemn and ritual, which can scarcely be joked about. When I occasionally suggest that it's a very expensive form of self-indulgence he is pained and shocked. Are all shooting-fans like that? I see no reason why people shouldn't do it (or hunting) if they like, but I can't quite swallow all their stuff about its being good for the birds and foxes. Or are you so ancestrally deep in the *mystique* that you think me iconoclastic?

23 September 1959   *Grundisburgh*

I spent a long evening after finishing my last G.C.E. paper (the author of which had the impressive name of Amelia Macdoom) reading *The Lion* from beginning to end, and relishing it vastly. I suppose the reviewers are right in saying the mystical and the factual are inade-

---

[1] Matthew Arnold, 'To Marguerite, continued'.

quately blended, but I got several good thrills out of it. The first encounter with King left me literally breathless. The author conveys —as Blake did in 'The Tiger'—the deadly terror roused when his eyes changed 'from soft gold to a glacial yellow,' and makes the dealings of the girl with King entirely convincing. I was sorry when he had to die.

You will be amused to hear that my nephew's gesture apropos of Stevenson's tombstone *did* produce a letter of protest in a New Zealand paper on the grounds that there were many causes worthier of £50, and the inscription as it stood did adequate justice to its subject. Charles hasn't stopped foaming at the mouth since he saw the letter. I have replied by pointing out that, though not at first sight strongly resembling Mary Magdalene, he is being misjudged exactly in the same way as she was over that spikenard. I remember a young Socialist years ago condemning Shakespeare as valueless because 'he wrote nothing about the class-war'. But is it only senile pessimism on my part which sees the defence of worth-while values becoming a tougher job every year?

To-morrow we go to listen to our sitting Tory. I didn't want to, but Pamela insists. I think she sees me being tarred and feathered by the local diehards if I don't go. I hope he will be heckled.

I giggle over what Adam left behind—as cheering evidence that boys don't alter. Braces and the Chess Club money are supremely right. Was it in your day that the Hon. Sec. of the Shakespeare Society took the minute-book with him to Cambridge, and Luxmoore had eventually to get the Cambridge police to extract it from him?

I didn't know Peter was a gun-fanatic. I never was, but there were a good many in Worcestershire in the early 1900's. A man who shot accidentally a young pheasant in September was not actually cut by the county but apt to be vaguely referred to as 'poor Tom', the underlying inference being that he couldn't be 'all there'. There is a very good scene in a book of R.H. Benson's, *The Conventionalists*, describing the awful solemnity with which the 'veterans of the smoking-room' discuss the 'problem of the second barrel'. The host presides, with great tact and geniality while chiefly engaged in 'smoking a cigar as well as it could be smoked'. R.H.B. could do such episodes superbly, but I expect he was before your day. Like hunting-men and foxes, shooters, without actually averring that the pheasant enjoys being shot at, are quite sure that the bird if offered the choice of living to be shot or not living at all, would vote for the former. Ask Peter.

At the library yesterday I picked up a book called something like *The Craft of Letters*, a symposium in which John Lehmann put the *Life of Hugh Walpole* at the top of modern biographies, so there!

I must stop. My doctor this morning thought to reassure me about the itch with the information that 'the skin is one and indivisible', which I thought was only said of God and peace. But at least it seems to mean that there is every hope that my ailment is *not* leprosy. I am rather like C.M. Wells (now 88) who was always convinced that every ache spelt cancer or paralysis, and every sneeze pneumonia.

27 September 1959   *Bromsden Farm*

Once again the hot sunshine kept me out in the garden all day, and I am behindhand with everything, so you won't get much of a letter, I fear. I have just finished reading Gissing's surviving letters to H.G. Wells. I suppose I shall publish them, but truly they're very dull— which I fear is the epithet that fits all Gissing's work. Have you read any of his novels?

No reviews of Jonah yet: it's just as well he doesn't get back from Italy till the end of next week. Did I tell you that he's now trying his hand at short stories? He simply can't stop writing, has exhausted his memories, knows that no-one will publish his books on religion, is tired of verse, and so falls back on fiction. What will it be like?

So glad you enjoyed *The Lion*: didn't you think the opening very good: all the animals in the morning?

I can see you're going to be much more involved in the Election than I am. I love the way you say 'sitting Tory', as though he were something protected by decent feeling, like a sitting pheasant. I fancy I have inadvertently disfranchised myself by failing to apply in time for a postal vote, but Henley's Tory is safely sitting and won't miss my X.

The Craft of Letters was *edited* by John Lehmann, but the gratifying remarks in it about my book were by J.I.M. Stewart, a Christ Church don who writes excellent detective stories as Michael Innes.

Let me tell you of my latest piece of Oscar-hunting. In 1929 an incredibly addle-witted society woman called Mrs Claude Beddington published a rubbishy book of memoirs, full of wind, famous names and split infinitives. In the middle of it she irrelevantly printed four excellent letters from Oscar to someone called 'Harry', written in 1885. Seeing Mrs C.B.'s name in the telephone book, I wrote to her (she must be very old) asking if she had the original letters, and whether she could now tell me who Harry was. No answer, so I rang up. She proved to be a vitriolic old tartar: 'I certainly shan't tell you who he was, no matter how often you ask me!' She then wrote me an abusive letter, accusing me of 'stirring up muck' to make money, which seemed a little hard since after all she printed these letters first. Nettled by the old bitch, I determined to find out Harry's name without her. The only clues in the letters were that he had been a Bluecoat Boy and was up at Cambridge in November 1885. I wrote to a dear old man at Christ's Hospital (retired beak, now in charge of the library, met through Edmund Blunden) asking if he could give me a list of Old Blues who were at Cambridge in November '85, and had Harry or Henry as Christian name. Back in a quaking hand came the answer: 'There was only one—H.C. Marillier (1865–1951)'. This was a great stroke of luck, and a glance at *Who Was Who* showed that he was clearly my man. But I still wanted the originals, so while I was busy Ruth went down to Somerset House and looked at his will. He left everything to his second wife, and the will was witnessed by 'Ernest H. Pooley, Barrister'. This rang a bell, and sure enough I found in *Who's Who* that Sir Ernest Pooley married in 1953 the widow of H.C. Marillier!

All this happened last week, and on Friday I wrote to Lady Pooley, asking whether she had the original letters, and if there were more (Mrs Beddington in our telephone duel told me that 'Harry' had a suit-case full!). I can't wait to get her answer. Meanwhile Mrs Beddington, softened by the reasonable answer I sent her, shows signs of weakening, but I'd love to be able to tell her that I not only know who Harry was, but have got the originals. See what a lot of time I enjoyably waste!

Mrs Beddington seemed to think that to have received a letter from Oscar would brand anyone as a pervert down the ages. I told her

I had letters to 250 men and women, including Browning, Gladstone, Matthew Arnold, Irving, Ellen Terry, Whistler, Bernard Shaw, Ruskin etc etc, and she really couldn't think them *all* queer. Harry, she told me, was '200% normal' (sounds terrifyingly unbalanced, doesn't it?) and twice married. 'Why do you worry then?' said I.

Goodnight, dear George, another exciting instalment next week.

1 October 1959   *Grundisburgh*

The majestic splendours of September's passing equalled or even surpassed its incomparable prime. Lord's at 4.30 yesterday afternoon was not a cricket-ground of this world, though the committee-room was earthly enough. Poor old Plum really does 'mop and mow' now. Does the passage of time really insist on a jaw that wags and wags, and that eyelids shall be rimmed with geranium-red? I am not sure they were not more sensible in medieval times when the holy maul was kept behind the church-door with which to brain the senile when they were beyond a joke. *Pro tem.* and judging by what daughters and friends say, I *am* a joke, so nothing need be done for a year or two.

Gissing I read quite a lot of fifty years ago. Dreary stuff I seem to remember, except—*what* was that book called he wrote when at last he wasn't starving? I then thought it rather beautiful, but haven't seen it for years.[1] The late Headmaster of Wolverhampton, one Warren Derry, an amiable and definitely intelligent man, has nearly finished a life of Dr Parr.[2] He thought of approaching the O.U.P. but is rather off it. I told him I would tell you about it. Not that I held out any hopes, but said, which is true, that it sounded a book which would interest you. He told me some very good things about the old pedant. But I expect you have your own plans and are up to the neck for years.

Your Oscar episode is absorbingly interesting—a rare piece of comedy ending with your discovery of Harry's identity, Lady Pooley and the weakening of Mrs Beddington. Mind you tell me all the rest

[1] Probably *By the Ionian Sea* (1901).
[2] The Rev. Samuel Parr (1747–1825), schoolmaster at Harrow, where he taught Sheridan, and other schools. Voluminous writer, in Latin and English, on politics and religion.

as it happens. After all some day these letters of yours to me will be a largely complete autobiography. Very few such have any stories so good. And there are plenty of others.

I remember Roger being as indignant as he can be (which is nothing much!) at old Queen Mary and George VI objecting to his mentioning that Q. Victoria's dress on a certain occasion was too low. ('Why lug this in?' H.M. pencilled in the margin.) It had already appeared un-objected-to in print: Greville, I guess.

I came back from Cambridge yesterday where I was for one night at a hotel in a garden bordering the river. There was a largish bade-lynge of ducks which one guest out of every three fed with bread. The ducks were clearly socialist ducks. Whenever one got a larger bit than the rest a dozen at once pursued her and tried to bag it. The possessor eluded them and won but only by dint of bolting the morsel, so in the end it did no good to anyone. I enjoyed the air of meek triumph which it assumed the moment after victory. You could *hear* it saying 'Sucks to you' (there is a pun somewhere here).

I am always amused at your reception of any name I suggest for the Lit. Soc. (not I grant you with any great conviction or partisan urging): so far they are either homos, or drunkards, or bores, or aesthetically (to eye or ear etc) repulsive, or all of these at once. Do you think my Extra Studies had somehow a homosexual influence? So many of my audience have gone that way. But it is of course well on the way, judging by our novelists, to becoming a *virtue*. Our philosophers appear to be agreed that there are no absolutes in morals, so the vice of one century may be the virtue of another.

Harry Altham, the new M.C.C. president, told me to-day that he has copied out and given to at least six people, old Jonah's poem on Eton in *A La Carte* and they are all thrilled by it. And no one has ever heard of it! Did not his publishers do pretty poorly about the book? As you know, it is of first-rate quality and the reviews said so when it came out. I feel dubious about his stories somehow, but who can tell? I wrote and told him how much I liked his book, but he won't have got it yet.

There was an excellent dinner-party here last night, and I particu-larly enjoyed a good crack with Joan Astley who is splendid company. I told her I was writing to you and she enjoined me to send you abundant good wishes. There was also a charming American lady, Mrs du Boulay, whom you may know—merely for the reason that there seem to be jolly few people you don't know.

How you will mock me when you hear that on leaving Cambridge temporarily bookless I spent half a crown on the Penguin *Lucky Jim* to see if on a second reading it was—as I thought—the earnest record of trivial people doing and saying trivial things, with no particular wit or felicity of style in the writing. And it is in its thirtieth edition—has a page of ecstatic press-statements about its brilliance. It might be the book the world is waiting for.

4 October 1959   *Bromsden Farm*

Do by all means suggest to Warren Derry that he should send me his life of Dr Parr, if possible without raising his hopes. Sparrow is a great expert on Parr, and if necessary I might get his advice. Although I am persistently overwhelmed by books and manuscripts, I never in fact have *enough*, and each time one of my half-yearly lists appears I wonder how on earth the next one is to be composed.

On Tuesday I got a charming answer from Lady Pooley (*çi-devant* Mrs Marillier) saying she had *no* O.W. letters and remembered her late husband (Harry) saying he had never had them back from Mrs Beddington! Accordingly I wrote to Mrs B, saying I now knew who Harry was, and that his widow believed Mrs B still had the letters, and wouldn't she have another look for them. No answer from her yet. Another good O.W. letter (to W.L. Courtney) turned up last week from a friend in America.

Did you see that the leading article in the current *Spectator* recommends its readers to vote Liberal, or failing that Labour? Surely there will be a flood of abuse and resignations from the far-flung rectories? I have already cast my True Blue vote by post, since I shall be in London on Polling Day. The *Daily Telegraph* is giving its usual all-night party in half the Savoy, with unlimited food, drink, dancing, and dreary results flashed onto a huge screen. I have been to two of them and shall avoid this one. My daughter Bridget, who is dying to go, is planning to get herself in on my invitation card.

And as for your endemic masochism—deliberately re-reading *Lucky Jim*—well! I look back in pity.

Summer-time, winter-time, it makes no difference to the delicious mid-day heat, and today I picked *sixty lbs* of quinces from our one tiny tree.

Last night Duff arrived back bronzed and cheerful after six weeks in Greece. He had driven a thousand miles in three days, but seemed none the worse. On Friday he returns to Oxford for his last year, and on Saturday plays for Fred's Old Boys against the Field. Adam says that none of the doors in the new house shut, and there is no hot water in the showers. He is now *Secretary* of the Chess Club, so some other boy's parents will have to stump up when the £3 in the tobacco-tin disappears.

Last week Ruth and I were taken to Graham Greene's play *The Complaisant Lover*, which we both enjoyed. Ralph Richardson gives an excellent performance in it.

When we meet on the 13th (Tommy, alas, can't come to the dinner) I shall have come almost straight from a committee-meeting of the London Library, at which a tricky question has to be answered. The Trustees of Carlyle's House in Chelsea (Harold Nicolson is one) have asked the Library to lend them for an indefinite period Carlyle's sofa and armchair, which for many years have stood in an obscure corner of the Library, unlabelled; indeed I doubt if half-a-dozen members even know they're there. Committee-members leave their hats and coats on them: that's all. My strong feeling is that they should go to Cheyne Row, where they will be seen and known (perhaps even admired) for what they are. Clearly H.N. will back me up, but the Librarian tells me there will be opposition. No doubt the impish Fulford will have a Liberal word to say. You shall hear all about it.

Next Saturday is the wedding, and Ruth is overwhelmed with pre-parations. It's at a village called Stoke-by-Nayland, beyond Colchester, and the expedition will take all day. Comfort is coming too, and my sister.

The electric drilling in Soho Square is jolly nearly insupportable: it has already been in progress for a month, curse them.

I copied out an incredible paragraph from the egregious Mrs Beddington's memoirs, but stupidly left it in London, so you'll have to wait a week for its doubtful pleasure.[1]

Peter's agent here—a nice active man of thirty-five—was stricken last Saturday with violent polio, and has been in an iron lung for a week, almost beyond hope. Now the fact that he has survived so long apparently brings a little hope. He has a wife and three small children. Adam and Bridget have been inoculated, but Duff never had his second jab, which I'm now ordering him to arrange immediately. I suppose one day they'll find a cure.

7 October 1959   *Grundisburgh*

How infallibly tiresome human beings can be—especially those who regard themselves as high-minded. Your wretched Mrs Bedding-ton of course should let you have all the O.W. letters she has apparently pinched. But she won't, having (as one reads between the lines) the wrongheaded obstinacy of such folk, half fool and half knave. Per-haps Lady Pooley could use legal pressure to get the letters? It is an engrossing story.

I *greatly* enjoyed Jonah's book, and wrote to tell him so; he has a delightful style—light and firm. But won't the chorus of indolent reviewers talk about waste-paper baskets, scraping the barrel, etc? So easy, now that the 'belles lettres' essay or causerie is out of fashion. Birkenhead, though, was quite pleasant in the *Sunday Times*. But he is an O.E. Kingsley Amis is not, and *Lucky Jim* is very unlike Jonah's work. I like your Maxian expression 'endemic masochism,' and plead guilty, secure in the comfortable knowledge that if and when your letters are published, practically nobody will know the meaning of either word. But I didn't spend much time over the vapid complica-tions of what it is putting it too high to call the love-affairs of some of

[1] 'Mrs Cornwallis-West's daughter, Shelagh, had married Lady Gros-venor's son, the present Duke of Westminster, and George Wyndham's brother, Guy, was the husband of Mrs Cornwallis-West's sister, Minnie; thus Mrs Cornwallis-West was the mother-in-law of Lady Grosvenor's son as well as the sister-in-law of Lady Grosvenor's husband.'
(Mrs Claude Beddington, *All That I have Met*, 1929, p. 171.)

the most insignificant and boring people that ever breathed. The grim truth is, however, that I am no nearer than before to solving the mystery of its immense success. But, as Birrell said, one needn't worry if modern stuff doesn't appeal, as there is always Boswell to read thoroughly. Do you know at all what happened at the Johnson Club meeting, at which grave matters were to be discussed? The club cannot go on as at present.

Of course that sofa and chair should be in Cheyne Row,[1] and why should anyone object? But of course they will. I hand you this from Bishop Creighton, which you may be able to use. 'After we have let the ape and tiger die in dealing with ourselves, there remains the donkey, a more intractable and enduring animal.' You could also say that a fellow-founder of the London Library with Carlyle has a grandson (G.W.L.) who is sure his grandfather would have approved of the transfer. How did the two things ever get to the Library? Are there relics of all the founders?

Stoke-by-Nayland is not at all far from here. I wish Ruth could look in here. She would refresh us far more than a week's rain for which we pant, but no doubt she has not a moment. Oh yes and of course you too; I hadn't realised you would be there. Stupid!

I think I grow steadily stupider. Last week I attended a committee-meeting of the Governing Bodies Association, and was bewildered by the ease and confidence with which portentous knights like Sir Griffith Williams and Sir William Cleary threaded their way among the intricacies of the English educational system. They really do know the difference between a direct-grant and a grant-aided school which to the normal man is as much a mystery as the difference between a Republican and a Democrat in the U.S.A. However *Who's Who* reveals that they have been in or about the Board of Education most of their lives, where I suppose such knowledge is essential. I now understand the slightly frosty look on the jowly visage of Sir Griffith when I said a certain action of the minister's apropos of Woodbridge School was 'bogus'. It is not impossible that he formulated it. My suspicion that I had put my foot in it was aroused by the impish grin on the Archbishop's face. I like his boyishness, though many no doubt would say archbishops should not be boyish. But it is an effective and lubricatory

[1] They now are.

element of his admirable chairmanship. He would be a better companion on a desert island than Sir Griffith.

Last night I began *Dr Zhivago*, but rather doubt if I shall persevere. I am *not* good at the Russians—'fluid puddings' as Henry James called their great novels. I don't understand *why* they say and do the things they do. I expect you took it in your stride and put it at the top of twentieth-century fiction. The plain truth is that I am too old, too dull-witted, too inattentive, too out of date. None the less I am coming to the Lit. Soc. on Tuesday. And I am writing to Warren Derry—when I can find his address.

Only a half-length letter to-day, alas, but I shall see you on Tuesday, and just now things are crowding in on me. All yesterday was taken up by the wedding of Ruth's son: all went well, and the bridegroom's mother looked exquisitely beautiful. It's too bad that we couldn't take advantage of our comparative nearness to you, but it wasn't possible.

At 10.30 tomorrow the Court of Appeal will begin its hearing of the London Library's rating-appeal, and I must be there to listen. After keeping us waiting fifteen months for a date, they finally gave us four days' warning. T.S.E. was (still is) on his way to America, but I managed to telephone to him in his cabin before the *Queen Mary* sailed, and he angelically said I could put his name to any letter I thought suitable for *The Times*. If we lose our appeal, it seems sensible to try and float our public appeal for money on the wave of sympathy which we shall surely receive, so there probably won't be time to send a draft letter to the U.S.A. for T.S.E.'s approval. This afternoon Simon Nowell-Smith and I roughed out a rather pedestrian first draft. They expect the hearing to end on Tuesday, and the London Library committee meeting is fixed for 2.45 that day. So I look like having a busy couple of days.

No answer from Mrs Beddington: I fear she has finally gone to ground. On Thursday evening I sat alone in the flat, unwillingly hypnotised by the election-results, which were mostly 'No Change' and pretty dull. I went to bed only when Gaitskell 'conceded' the election. So your gloomy forebodings were happily unjustified. Jonah came to see me and proudly showed me your letter, which was the first thing that greeted him on his return home from Italy and gave him untold pleasure. The Johnson Club meeting isn't till October 27, so those weighty issues remain undecided. I don't think I could use Bishop Creighton's excellent phrase at the London Library meeting without some member of the committee taking it personally. Did you hear of the parson who began his sermon: 'As God said—and rightly — . . .' It grows on one.

I have never attempted *Dr Zhivago*, and doubt whether I ever shall —so there!

All football was stopped at Eton last week, as each game on rock-hard ground produced a crop of broken bones.

15 October 1959   *Grundisburgh*

A *very* good evening again. And how well and svelte (*le mot juste!*) you were looking and how lovely was Ruth. We had good talk at our end. The wicked knight[1] was in excellent form (I am *not* referring to Tim!) and I am certain enjoyed himself. Jonah kept him well in play, but four or five joined in. Afterwards I had a talk with John Sparrow about Dr Parr and his prospective author, whom he knows quite well and approves of. And yesterday I wrote to Derry and encouraged him to get into touch with you—at the same time making it clear that he mustn't take your flawless affability and courtesy and interest as any sign that your professional judgment was bamboozleable (a *good* word. M. Banck was before your day at Eton who told his division, 'I stand no boozlebam from little English boys', with the result of course that he had to stand it—and much else—for the next eleven years.) Then Ivor, Jonah, Sparrow, and I sat until after 10.30, when all you sissies were tucking yourselves up. No, I exempt *you*, who never face less than two men's work every morning. An interesting point was that during the entire evening not *one* word was said about the election, though many topics were tossed about. Flash Harry bet Peter Fleming

[1] Sir Malcolm Sargent.

half a crown that the word 'spike*n*ard' does not come in the New Testament Mary Magdalene episode. Surely F.H. will lose. As the 'little judge' said in the Bardell case[1]: 'How could I have got it on my notes?' i.e. why do we know the word at all if it is in no gospel? He seems to know the Bible as well as he knows Beethoven—but he *didn't* know the saddest and shortest biography ever written, which is in it. I think I have told it to you. The late Lord Jowitt was delighted with it.

What does 'Judgment Reserved' mean? I hope that the holy three are putting their heads together to defeat the letter of the law—but I don't suppose I am more optimistic than you are. The law is so often a ass (only seven people in England ever quote Mr Bumble correctly —and I am one of them!).

The next case of any real interest may well be 'Lyttelton v. X.Y.Z.', to wit my solicitors, who have for a year and a half had £4500 of mine, from the redemption of some gilt-edged stock, and forgot either to ask my trustees about re-investing, or even putting it on deposit. Really men of law and business are more inept, careless, doodle-witted, opinionated and mendacious than parsons, schoolmasters and publishers!

18 October 1959   *Bromsden Farm*

Having had a delightful hour of you beforehand I can resign myself to the fact that it is so often the *other* end of the dinner-table that you are keeping a-roar. You were in splendid form on Tuesday, and clearly enjoying yourself, to my great delight. While you were hobnobbing with Sparrow and Co I had withdrawn to an upper chamber with the amenable Roger, and between us we re-wrote (for the fifth time) the draft letter to *The Times* about the London Library. 'Judgment Reserved' means that we shan't know the verdict for about a fortnight— which gives me time to send the draft letter to T.S.E. for a sixth revision by the master hand. I have asked Masefield to back up our letter with another on the following day, when the time comes. Roger

---

[1] In which Mr Pickwick's landlady Mrs Bardell successfully sued him for breach of promise. The little judge was Mr Justice Stareleigh (see *Pickwick Papers*, chapter xxxiii).

came to the Court of Appeal for the tail-end of the hearing on Wednesday morning. I hear rumours, through our solicitor, that our admirable Counsel, Geoffrey Lawrence, may charge nothing at all for this whole appeal! His normal fee would be about £700, so his waiving it would be a tremendously generous gesture: surely the least we could do would be to make him an honorary Life Member of the Library.[1]

On Wednesday the Court of Criminal Appeal was hearing the Podola case in the next court.[2] The wretched man himself wasn't there (for which Ruth was rather thankful), but we pushed our way through a phalanx of coal-black law-students and others to have a look at the court—and very impressive it was, with five judges in wigs and scarlet gowns ranged in line with the Lord Chief Justice in the middle. The Attorney General (that ass Manningham-Buller) was reading a mass of argument about 'true amnesia', but the scene was none the less dramatic. (A B.B.C. announcer has just said 'controversy—God help him!)

I fancy Flash Harry will lose his half-crown over spikenard, which, according to Cruden, occurs in two of the Gospels. I wouldn't have expected P.F. to know any more of the Bible than F.H. Please tell me (you never have) the saddest and shortest biography.

For goodness' sake take some firm steps to recover your £4500 before your solicitors abscond. The first solicitors I ever had to deal with bore the splendidly Dickensian name of Smith, Rundell, Dodds and Bockett. Don't you love the way it begins quietly with the simple Smith (clearly an alias) and works its way gradually into top gear with the improbable Bockett? J.M. Keynes said he considered solicitors as a class to be ignorant, stupid and ineffectual—and who are we to dispute the great man's word?

Peter looked in to-day. His agent is still (after three weeks) desperately ill with polio, and has to be artificially fed since he can't swallow. There's no knowing when or if he'll be able to work again, which is a great nuisance for Peter.

[1] We gratefully did.
[2] Guenther Fritz Podola, a German–Canadian, had murdered a police sergeant while on the run from a blackmail charge. He pleaded hysterical amnesia, but was convicted. His appeal was dismissed and he was executed on 5 November.

Fred's old boys were beaten 3–2 by the Field, and Duff scored the 2. He is now in digs at Oxford and planning to work for his Schools next June. He took a lot of excellent colour-photographs in Greece and is hoping to lecture with them at prep-schools for a fiver a time, as he successfully did after his Russian trip. We are encouraging him to apply for a Commonwealth Fellowship, which would mean a year at an American university.

Adam reports shamefacedly that the school were beaten at chess by Mill Hill!

I am now two-thirds of the way through *Past and Present*: some of it is pretty dull, but as always with T.C. there are memorable moments when the grumbling thunder gives place to a flash of lightning, and Abbot Samson is a nice new friend. I'm also much enjoying George Painter's new life of Proust, which is full of wit and scholarship. Ronald Knox and Queen Mary await my attention.

Did I tell you that last week I heard of twenty-five new Oscar letters in Texas?! Photostats are on their way, and expectation is high. It begins to look as though I shall print the best part of a thousand letters—but when? you ask, and my answer is an apologetic and explanatory mumble.

Sparrow told me at dinner that G.M. Young is now in an old men's home at Goring-on-Thames, quite gaga and not properly recognising Sparrow when he goes there: very sad, but it's a great relief not to have him at All Souls, as one can imagine.

Didn't you think Jonah looked very pale and old the other evening? I fear that pneumonia in the summer aged him a little. He is rather upset because Harold Nicolson hasn't reviewed his new book in the *Sunday Times* (nor has anyone else), and I try to comfort him.

On Friday I was drawn (or caricatured) for *Punch*: I'll let you know when the result is going to appear, but I daresay you see that dismal hebdomadal regularly. Last week I won a dictionary from the *Spectator* for solving their crossword—or rather Ruth did, for I always send in solutions in her name, so that she'll have the fun of getting the prize if there is one.

Have I missed Diana's baby in *The Times*, or hasn't it appeared yet? How many grandchildren will that make?

Goodnight, beloved patriarch. I must do some work.

As if whenever I glanced down *your* end of the table I didn't see one vast chuckle, every face a-wreath with smiles! Our roars were mainly the work of Jonah and Flash Harry, who was in fine salacious fettle. Yes, I did enjoy every moment, but then I always do. It is a warming thought to reflect what an amount of great and continuing happiness *you* have poured into my senescent years—letters, Lit. Soc., books, *Ruth*—isn't that a pretty good cornucopia? This very morning two lovely fat books, obviously bursting with good qualities. No return that I can make for these rich benevolences looks anything—*is* anything—but derisory in comparison. As Pamela said at breakfast, the luck of finding such generosity in the book-world just when reading is one's chief pleasure is simply fantastic.

I *do* hope you will defeat those brigands. I keep an eye wide open for your letter. A slightly less momentous one from me is in to-day's *Times*, which I expect you missed; it is shamefacedly tucked away on page 3. It will be interesting to see if anyone answers. It may light such a candle, Master Ridley, among all the more purpled and dew-lapped members of the M.C.C. Do you think that *all* the famous sayings, last words etc were invented? I have written to Plum Warner that my nephew said he was told by Rhodes that Trumper never said 'For God's sake Wilfred, give me a moment's peace' in the 1903 Test Match at Sydney, when V.T. made 185 and Rhodes bowled all afternoon on the plumbest of wickets; and I urged Plum to let us know the truth, which he must know.

Later. A postcard from Plum, mainly illegible, and the only decipherable thing is that *none* of any of the sayings attributed to cricketers is true. We must fall back on old Agate's view that there are two truths to everything—factual and artistic, the first being what *did* happen and the second what *ought* to have happened, or alternatively what Achilles actually did, and what Homer recorded his doing. Agate's great example of this theory was Cardus's superb description of Tom Richardson at Old Trafford in 1896—T.R. standing dazed, like some great animal, by the failure of his heroic effort—the factual truth being that when the winning hit was made he was legging it to the pavilion and had downed his quart before anyone else had got there.

Geoffrey Lawrence sounds a good man. Why are barristers usually spirited and interesting chaps and solicitors exactly the opposite? I don't think mine will abscond—yet, anyway. My brother is hot on their trail. The head of the firm is straight out of Dickens or Wells. He bites his thumb, not as a sign of contempt but to give him an air of deep thought; he makes notes about what one is saying on his blotting-paper, and once, I know, there was certainly no lead in his pencil (may I remind you of the Staffordshire squire who begat an heir when over seventy and mocked at the disappointed heir-apparent for 'thinking I had no lead in my pencil'. Hush!).

I like the names of your first solicitors. All in jail now I suppose? They are almost in the class of Quirk, Gammon, and Snap in Warren's *Ten Thousand a Year*. My father had an old friend whose name had the reverse trend—a majestic start—and a weak finish. Ferdinando Dudley Lee Smith. But Keynes was right. Solicitors are always getting wrong exactly what we pay them—rather heavily—*not* to get wrong, e.g. wills. My uncle Bob was a solicitor—and far the stupidest of all the eight brothers. He did all the family business and cost them thousands through his blundering. Still, I recollect with gratitude an item on the bill he sent my cousin: 'To conversation on telephone about Captain X's pension, and agreeing that it would be a small one: £1. 6. 8.' I class that with Pamela's bill from a vet 'to attendance on cat 1/6; to removal of cat 1/-; to burial of cat 1/6 = £0. 4. 0.' Which brings me to Jehoiachin. Look up *II Chronicles* xxxvi, 9, because if I merely quote you won't believe me.[1] You will be interested; so will Ruth (and I suspect, that like me, it will move her just a *little* way in the direction of tears!). What *could* the poor imp have done? I suppose he catapulted the postman's dog or something of the sort. It must be admitted that the same king in the *Book of Kings* is given *eighteen* years, but no one has thought of correcting *Chronicles*, and there it remains. I imagine the

---

[1] 'Jehoiachin was eight years old when he began to reign, and he reigned three months and ten days in Jerusalem: and he did that which was evil in the sight of the Lord.'

poor lamb was knocked on the head after a reign of three months and ten days—just about a Michaelmas half.

Jonah writes cheerfully, but says he is being kept indoors for breathlessness, which doesn't sound too good. He *did* look rather battered on Tuesday, but was in good form and stayed late.

I hope the dictionary Ruth won was the thirteen-volume Oxford. But probably you have that. I could never run to it.

Yes, Diana's second son turned up *on* the day (characteristic!) and all goes well. And Rose reports No 5 should appear in April (our nineteenth. At the moment it is nine boys, nine girls, and *all* sound in wind, limb, *and* mind. There is no 'poor Dorothy' thank God).

Yes, of course a lot of *Past and Present* is entirely out of date now. But as you say, through all the dead grey lava the old volcano sometimes erupts finely. Abbot Samson is alive all right, also Willelmus Sacrista and his potations. Little things stick in my memory, Richard's 'tornado' oaths and a tiny snapshot of John 'in cramoisie velvet', was it? And you know there are some jolly good things in his fierce *Latter-Day Pamphlets*. *All* the abuses of government, Parliament etc which he savages are still alive. Read—it won't take you two minutes—the Pig Philosophy in the article 'Jesuitism' and say if you can that we have outgrown all that. And on lots of other pages he might be talking of the late d-d General Election!

I have just been reading about Courvoisier[1] and Wallace in the book of Mrs Yseult Bridges, who fancies her detections.[2] I suppose there cannot be much doubt that Wallace did kill his wife, but the Appeal Court were surely right. The evidence just fell short in point after point—but only just. Wallace's face gives *me* the shudders. Surely those eyes are not those of a sane man. I am sorry for Adam's sake that W. was a very keen chess-player. No Mill Hill champion would have beaten him! Mrs B hints that his murdering Mrs W. may have been

---

[1] François Benjamin Courvoisier, a Belgian valet, murdered his employer Lord William Russell in May 1840 and was publicly hanged outside Newgate prison on 6 July. Thackeray was taken to the execution and was so distressed by it that he wrote a strong anti-death-penalty article 'On Going to see a Man Hanged', which was published in *Fraser's Magazine*.

[2] *Two Studies in Crime* (1959).

in his eyes like a chess-problem, i.e. to block all police-moves as Alekhine foresaw and frustrated all moves his opponent might make. Will that wash?[1]

A splendid four-pager, with a two-page rider this week. I can't conceal from you the fact that Jonah's book isn't selling anything like as well as its predecessor, though I try to blur the facts to Jonah himself by vaguely encouraging noises. Still, he has had a pretty good run with his reminiscences, and I never expected great sales for this volume.

No news yet of the Court of Appeal's decision—and, more tiresome, no answer from T.S.E. in America. I have a nasty feeling that the whole thing will break between 2.30 on Wednesday (when I attend my first B.B.C. General Advisory Council Meeting) and 2.30 on Thursday, when I address the burghers of Preston on Francis Thompson. A busy week seems likely.

I think all the bright law-students must go to the Bar, leaving their duller brethren to be solicitors. I imagine that few barristers would get very far without some of those qualities which solicitors so signally lack.

Jehoiachin's story is certainly pitiful: I will give Ruth the reference tomorrow. No, I haven't got the big Oxford Dictionary, but the firm gave one to Arthur Ransome in reward for much help, and he has left it to me in his will, he says. I hope that many years will pass before I get it, since I am A.R.'s literary executor designate, and I don't want any more work just now.

So glad Diana's baby arrived safely: what a brood you have engendered!

---

[1] In 1931 William Herbert Wallace, a Liverpool insurance agent, was convicted of battering his wife to death, but the evidence was purely circumstantial, and the Court of Criminal Appeal quashed the verdict on the ground that it could not be supported, having regard to the evidence. Wallace died two years later, a broken man.

I obediently read and enjoyed 'Pig Philosophy', and am still wading through *Past and Present*.

Yesterday we drove to the Cotswolds to lunch with Comfort's stepmother, and afterwards I spent a delightful hour with Katie Lewis. She is 81, daughter of the first Sir George Lewis, the solicitor, and the only person I know who actually knew Oscar. True, she was only a child, but her memory is excellent, and since she seems to have known everybody since, she is splendid company. Just now she is mourning old Berenson, to whom she was devoted. Her parents were close friends of the Burne-Joneses, and her house is full of his pictures, as well as others, including a fine Rossetti drawing of Mrs William Morris. I wished I could have stayed longer. On the way we stopped for half-an-hour in Oxford and I snapped up a few secondhand books at Blackwell's. In term-time now it's almost impossible to park a car anywhere in the centre of the city: I suppose Cambridge is almost as bad. Nor will any number of ring-roads help to solve this problem. But driving in this country simply isn't fun any more: the wide deserted roads of France are another matter.

I'm just finishing the manuscript of a book I shall certainly publish. It's the first volume of the autobiography of John Morris, who recently retired from being Head of the Third Programme. It's an unusual book and he an unusual man. A contemplative recluse-type, he spent most of his life as an officer in the Indian Army (Gurkhas) and was on the first Everest expedition (1922). He is—or was—homosexual, and he treats this subject explicitly, with quiet dignity and good sense. I think it will interest you. It's called *Hired to Kill*—from Swift: 'A *Soldier* is a *Yahoo* hired to kill in cold Blood as many of his own species, who have never offended him, as he possibly can'.

But you know that already. If only all manuscripts were as acceptable! I rather look forward to the train-journeys to and from Preston, as undisturbed times for reading, though on the way up I shall doubtless be desperately preparing my speech. Why on earth did I ever agree to go? Ruth says I'm congenitally unable to say NO, but I *am* getting better at telling swift lies to telephoning hostesses, and long only to be left alone.

The Duff Cooper Prize for this year is looming up, and goodness knows who we can get to give it away. So far we've had Winston, the

Queen Mum and Princess Margaret: where do we go from there? Perhaps Diana will have an idea. Her second grandchild is expected daily—in Beirut, where the expectant father is recovering from amoebic dysentery. Now I must finish John Morris.

29 October 1959   *Grundisburgh*

I think you are right about solicitors and barristers. My uncle Bob would have been a hopeless barrister. It is true he was a hopeless solicitor too, but his firm didn't go bankrupt and he remained in it. He would have been disbarred in no time. He had in his prime a certain flair for words (e.g. Cobden's match[1]) and he loved rolling over his tongue words like 'reversionary legatee' though the family suspected he didn't know what either of them meant.

We go in a fortnight or so to *Trial by Jury* and *Pinafore*. I am President of the local G. and S. Society and have just written 250 words to be printed in the programme. *T. by J.* I haven't seen for over fifty years and remember thinking not very good. I am surprised too to find that *Pinafore* had a longer run first go than any of them (700 nights. *Mikado* came next with 672, but easily beat *P*. in all the revivals). What a tedious man Gilbert must have been—always in a huff about something, and brandishing his solicitor in every other letter.

What a pity the horse-whip is out of fashion. Did you ever know it used? I did—on an (eventually) eminent civil servant who jilted an old-fashioned and hot-tempered man's sister. I still meet him at Lord's sometimes. He is riddled with arthritis and couldn't horse-whip a mouse now.

You must have had a good spell with Sir George Lewis's daughter who 'saw Shelley plain', so to speak. Wasn't O.W. great fun with children, or did I imagine that? My hat, there will be good reading in your book when it comes. *Will* it come? Remember, as warning, the Balzac story in which an artist spent so long perfecting his picture that it ended as an almost complete blur, save for one tiny foot of breath-

[1] His stirring account of the University Match of 1870, published in the Badminton Library volume *Cricket* (1888), edited by A. G. Street and the Hon. R. H. Lyttelton.

taking loveliness.[1] But surely it *must* be a best-seller on both sides of the Atlantic: or have tastes been finally corrupted by *Lucky Jim* and *Rooms at the Top*?

Have you ever picked up a real bargain at Blackwell's or Foyle's? John Bailey haunted the Charing Cross Road for years, but had no luck, till one day in Paris he picked up a book of poems with on the fly-leaf 'William Wordsworth from his friend Robert Southey'. I don't know what happened to it.

John Morris is new to me, but *Hired to Kill* sounds good. Did you ever read Taine on Swift with his 'terrible wan eyes'? Taine is very vivid—superb on the Elizabethans, but completely mystified by the English admiration of Dr Johnson. He would be. The leading miller of Ipswich recently announced in the Club that 'Dr Johnson was a bore —not that I ever read Boswell of course'. Yes the horse-whip ought certainly to be revived.

All Saints Day 1959   *Bromsden Farm*

Jonah looked in on Friday, less pale and gaunt than he was at the Lit. Soc., but still very breathless and able to mount the stairs only one at a time with a rest between (it's a mercy he wasn't bound for the flat!). His doctors tell him that his heart and lungs are fine, and perhaps some form of anaemia is his trouble. Meanwhile he is hard at work writing short stories: what will they be like? He is being most good-natured and philosophical about the moderate sales of his last book.

Each time you mention Gilbert & Sullivan I confess that I have never witnessed any one of their works, but clearly you think I exaggerate. How can I convince you? Wagner, yes, but my parents cared nothing for G. and S., and no close friend or chance circumstance has since lit up my ignorance. I've read most of the *libretti* and heard all the music, but an opera in a theatre—no. Clearly I should repair this omission, grit my teeth, and go to the whole lot, one after the other,

[1] In Balzac's *Chef-d'Oeuvre Inconnu* there is no loveliness left. '*Je ne vois là [dit Poussin] que des couleurs confusément amassées et contenues par une multitude de lignes bizarres qui forment une muraille de peinture.*'

next time they're in London, but shall I? Perhaps *Patience*, with its Oscarian allusions, would set me rolling down the slippery slope?

I'd adore to see your arthritic old friend trying to horsewhip a mouse, after limbering up by breaking a few butterflies on the wheel.

Oscar was indeed excellent with children, but then he was excellent with everyone, and all fell beneath his spell—even as I have fallen, sixty years after his death. Yes, the book will definitely appear, though I still can't say exactly when.

My best bargain at Foyle's was a copy of Edward FitzGerald's (anonymous) *Readings in Crabbe*, inscribed by him to a friend. I got it for sixpence. In the old days on the Farringdon Road barrows (which nowadays I have no time to visit) I was always finding for sixpence or a shilling books worth several pounds, and I can still remember the first edition (four vols, one shilling each) of *Middlemarch*, which I had to leave because I could carry no more. Next day, not unnaturally, they had gone.

I have accepted *Hired to Kill* and am now preparing the manuscript for the printer—a wearisome task.

My first meeting of the General Advisory Council of the BBC was rather amusing. Imagine a huge Council Chamber, arranged like this:

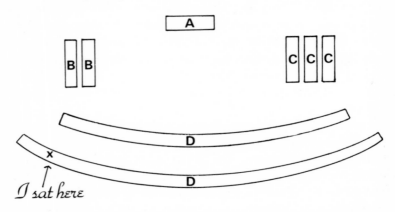

A. housed the Chairman (Norman Fisher—very good), Sir A. fforde (Chairman of Governing Body) and Sir I. Jacob (retiring Director General)

C. Massed BBC executives.

B. Governors

D. The Council.

I sat with two other 'new boys', Andrew Devonshire and Margaret Lane (Lady Huntingdon). A lot of questions (some interesting) were asked and more or less answered. The people who spoke most were Lord Strang (ex F.O. and very twitchy), a retired Governor of Nigeria called Sir James Mackintosh, Sir Hugh Linstead M.P., George Woodcock (of the T.U.C.), that horrible Patrick Gordon-Walker, the Bishop of Manchester, a chap called Hoare (something to do with the Cinema), Prof Mansergh (on Commonwealth relations) and, I'm delighted to say, Mr Gentle, head of the Greyhound Racing Association. When I crept away after two hours it was still going strong. Thelma Cazalet was the only Governor I knew. Gubby Allen is no longer on the Council.

On Wednesday, armed with sandwiches and coffee provided by Ruth, I travelled to Preston: the train was exactly an hour late. I stayed at the Victoria & Station Hotel (which must clearly take second place to the Hotel of the Immaculate Conception & the Post Office at Lourdes) and next day was lunched heavily by the (female) mayor and a mass of aldermen. Afterwards I spoke for half an hour in the Public Library to an audience of two hundred or so. Since my talk was almost purely literary, and most of them were utterly illiterate, little pleasure was enjoyed, except by the Library staff, who had arranged the Francis Thompson manuscripts and books most intelligently. (F.T. was born in Preston in 1859.) Sadly clutching a ham roll and a bar of chocolate I travelled back to London in a state of exhaustion.

5 November 1959   *Grundisburgh*

I can tell from my own feelings pretty well how angry you must be feeling about this Philistine triumph as the nice contemptuous little leader in *The Times* puts it. Shall you appeal to the House of Lords, or are they bound to say the same? How damnable it all is. English civilisation *deserves* to go down the drain. I hope Hodson[1] in his summing-up showed both sympathy and shame.

Jonah's health doesn't sound very good to me, who preserve the old belief that oarsmen's hearts are apt to go pop. I wonder how anaemia can cause breathlessness. What odd remote causes they

---

[1] Charles Hodson (b. 1895), then a Lord Justice of Appeal.

discover nowadays. I have occasional itching on elbow and ear. It is being put right by my wearing elastic stockings, believe it or not. I feel dubious about dear Jonah's short stories. So do you!

Odd your never seeing a Gilbert and S. play. Too late now, I suspect. Gilbert's prose is dreadful, and Sullivan's tunes are widely held to be 'twee'. They asked me to write 250 sparkling words on G. and S. for the *Pinafore* and *Trial by Jury* performances next week. I sent them (and thought they were rather good!) and have had neither acknowledgment, nor thanks. These are the times that try men's souls! Are you as aware as I am of the very strong movement in favour of *not* answering letters, *not* acknowledging, *not* thanking? It grows apace (I am reminded of a candidate who in a recent G.C.E. exam wrote in a *Richard II* paper that 'Bolingbroke was fond of trying not to annoy people'. (N.B. If you do go to a G. and S. play choose *Patience*, *Iolanthe*, or *Mikado*.)

Your B.B.C. General Advisory Council sounds from its personnel 'fine confused feeding'. No doubt whatever sensible and civilised measures you advocate will be turned down. Your vignette of Lord Stamp ('ex F.O. and very twitchy') brings him out very clearly—like Carlyle's Secretary the long-suffering Foxton, described by his master as 'very talky, scratch o'plastery, but good, compared with nothing'.

I see by the way that the rating of Lord's is probably going the same way as the London Library's. The M.C.C. want it to be £3500, the rating brigand £9000 odd, fortified no doubt by someone's suggestion (roughly) that a single-wicket match between Marilyn Monroe and Diana Dors would fill the stands. How I do hate all jacks-in-office—as you must have hated the Preston audience. But that in its turn may be senile pessimism. Books do seem to be increasingly read; they cannot all be drivel. A fan of Ian Fleming's said I *must* read his last one, and I did, but—! I.F.'s recipe is cards, wines and dishes (as costly as possible), torture, a seasoning of breasts and thighs, and a series of ludicrous strokes of luck and escapes by that very unattractive Bond from impasses in which his chief, who may have eyes of chilled steel and jaw of ditto, but certainly has a brain of cotton-wool, is always landing him. Can one really shoot a man in the back while playing baccarat in a crowded casino, without anyone hearing or suspecting till the murderer has vanished? What does P.F. think of I.F.'s books?

Last month my pre-Lit. Soc. letter missed you, so this time I plan
to post on Sunday. To-day the country seems to have been swathed
in fog, except just here, where we had bright hot sunshine all day. At
noon I sat outside reading, with no summer-house to protect me.
Adam is home for Long Leave: we are mercifully absolved from St
Andrew's Day this year, since Adam is largely in charge of a 'Con-
versazione' which is being laid on in the Science Schools, and is unwilling to be disturbed. One of the highlights, I gather, is to be a
working still, supplied by Guinness, with stout for the assistants.
Adam seems quite happy in the new house, but says that the boys
definitely don't get enough to eat.

The final scene in the Court of Appeal was on the drab side: since
one can appeal only on points of law, the verdict is purely legal, without occasion for sympathy or shame. Although our two main (and
vital) points were disallowed, so that a further appeal to the House of
Lords is pointless, two minor points were given in our favour, and
may well be a great help to other bodies in similar plight. (1) They
ruled that the word 'annual' in the phrase 'annual voluntary con-
tributions' could refer to the recipient, so that legacies can be included,
provided one can show a settled pattern of such receipts. (2) They
agreed that to a library a gift of books is just as much a 'contribution'
as a gift of money. These are two basic changes in the law, for which
others may bless us.

After the verdict I asked an usher if there was a room in which I
could have a brief consultation with the Librarian, our solicitor, etc.
He said 'You can go in here', and ushered us into THE LORD CHIEF
JUSTICE OF ENGLAND'S COURT (as was proclaimed by the entrance).
In these impressive surroundings we licked our wounds and decided
to put in motion the appeal for money. We received just over £1000 in
the first twenty-four hours after the letter in *The Times*, which seems
quite hopeful. This included another £400 from Donald Somervell,
bless him (he has had to have a second operation and is now in a
Canterbury hospital). Masefield's letter I kept up my sleeve, so as to
get it printed on the following day. I hope that the leading article on
the book-page of next Thursday's *Times* will be devoted to the Library,

and the *Guardian* rang me up yesterday about a piece they are preparing. I'm sure the great thing is to get as much publicity as we can as quickly as possible. I am having two thousand offprints of our *Times* letter, to use as ammunition. All this takes up a lot of time and energy.

In the middle of it I dashed to Broadcasting House and recorded three minutes' worth of drivel about Jonathan Cape's eightieth birthday. This you can hear tomorrow week (Sunday 15th) in a programme called The World of Books, though it will, as they say, bore the pants off you.

My writing is getting illegible—it wasn't Lord Stamp but Lord STRANG who twitched at that meeting.

I'm sure I warned you that Ian Fleming's last book was pretty poor: Peter is the soul of fraternal loyalty in these matters.

Yesterday morning I discovered, after months of patient tracking, that a Pall Mall bookseller has got nine excellent Wilde letters (which, ironically enough, I sold in Hugh Walpole's library at Christie's in 1945. Then they fetched £50, and now the bookseller wants £1000 for them). I went along to see him and he let me read the letters: at least two of them are first-rate, and somehow I *must* get them for my book (the bookseller would rather sell them as 'unpublished' and so is unwilling to let me copy them). I have already written to an American millionaire (who bought some other letters so that I could see them) and am hoping I can find a purchaser somewhere. How this book does grow! I'm still waiting for the final two batches of photostats from California.

Last week I was also much plagued by visiting American professors —three of them in one day left me breathless and exhausted. All nice and learned chaps, you know, but better taken in small doses.

Ruth won another crossword prize of 15/- last week, and since she and I have now received prizes from four papers lately, I've started sending in solutions with my sister's name and address.

I am told that *Queen Mary* and *Lolita* (blest pair of sirens) are carrying all before them in the bookshops, and we petty men must walk under their huge sales and peep about to find ourselves dishonourable graves. (Adam has just returned proudly bearing a partridge, after a day's shooting with friends.)

The Duff Cooper Memorial Prize is looming up again, and I am endeavouring, by very remote control, to snaffle Princess Alexandra as presenter.

N.B. PROBATE, DIVORCE AND ADMIRALTY DIVISION

CHINESE MARRIAGE DECLARED VALID

WOU v. WOU (WOU OTHERWISE COLLINGWOOD INTERVENING)

WOU (OTHERWISE COLLINGWOOD) v. WOU

12 November 1959   *As from Grundisburgh*

Again an excellent evening—though less good as lacking the hour beforehand. The old acid drop[1] was in pretty good fettle on the whole, though he wasn't going to admit approval of much. He said, *inter alia*, that I was very deaf (untrue), that the Lit. Soc. now mainly consisted, as far as he could see, of novelists whom nobody read (untrue), that, yes, Donald Somervell was a nice enough chap—but he saved his face by adding 'he was a very bad Attorney General' (probably untrue, and I thought of the equally sour Housman, when told that X said he was the best Latinist in Europe: 'That is not true, and if it were, X would not know it'). The flavour of Tommy's conversation on the other side had the additional freshness of contrast—a nutty claret after quinine. And what a nice fellow Alan Moorehead is. I like to meet a chap who really does take the fall in the hippopotamus population to heart.

Roger bustled off earlyish, having promised to see home Harold Nicolson whom he described as 'very tottery'. Do you agree? Jonah was momentarily deprived of breath on rising from the table, Bob Brand had special dishes all through the meal, and as I told you, Sir C. would describe me as deaf as a haddock.

What a foul city you live in! To breathe this afternoon is to inhale vaporised pennies—old ones. Everyone was delayed in getting to the Abbey School G.B. meeting and I had to take the chair. Like all school G.B. meetings the main topic was finance, but one item of the agenda was the rather incongruous one, for what sum should we sell the

[1] Cuthbert Headlam.

159

stuffed head of a bison which we mysteriously acquired with a recently bought house? I did what I could to keep them dallying with this, and just when short-term mortgages were looming, thank God the Chairman arrived and the bison was indefinitely consigned to limbo.

I am intrigued by Adam's temporary entry into the world of stout. Bid him remember that it is a *food*, and a barrel in his room will at least keep starvation at bay. Why should Fred's cook produce less food in the new house than she did in the old? School diet is a constant headache, though there is, I gather, a less unanimous conspiracy by all boys to say the food is 'muck' than there used to be. At a girls' school I know, the general cry always has been that the girls are not given enough to eat. But in the same breath the complainers admit that their daughters are radiant with health and energy and happiness. So what ought we to do? A century hence perhaps the faculty will be saying that eggs and bacon are the main cause of cancer, consumption, rheumatism and corns. But I hope they will last my time. Do I know your *bêtes noires*? I think I should. Mine are parsnips, artichokes, Brussels sprouts, ginger, boiled mutton, macaroni, sago, skate, pike, and whale—not only because Dr Summerskill recommended it, though that could surely be held ample reason.

I am in the middle of the Druon book[1] and after a slow start, enjoying it. But do they really copulate as much as that in France—or die so frequently? And I wanted to ask you about *Lolita*. Need I read it? *Dr Zhivago* smothered me before half-way. And tell me all about Middleton Murry, whom no doubt you knew. Dislike of D.H. Lawrence makes me incline to like M.M. but I suppose he *was* a rum cuss. Not, surely, a very bad critic of Shakespeare, Keats and Co., at his best? But 'everything by starts and nothing long.'[2]

I turn steadily into Mr Pooter. Yesterday evening I bent to light a spill and a shout of ribald laughter announced that the seat of my trousers had a rent in it, one of those silent unannounced rents that come to thirty-year-old trouser-seats just before they give up the ghost. Has it ever happened to you? I inherit it. My mother used to send my father's oldest clothes to jumble bazaars in Worcestershire. My father used to visit the sale and buy them all back. Charles Fisher

---

[1] *The Curtain Falls* by Maurice Druon.
[2] Dryden, *Absalom and Achitophel*.

(killed at Jutland) and a friend found a jacket of my cousin Ted Talbot's at the tailor's, sent for cleaning. They got hold of a handful of buttons, two small bits of old cloth, and some shreds and patches, borrowed the tailor's note-paper and sent the stuff up to Ted T. saying 'Dear Sir, We regret to inform you that after cleaning the enclosed articles are all that remains of your jacket'. A good joke I think. Please agree.

Surely *some* very rich man will buy really worthwhile immortality by establishing the London Library. An American?? It *cannot* be allowed to fade away or even alter. Your (and T.S.E.'s) letter was a very good one. So was Masefield's.

Shall you tell anywhere the whole story of the Wilde letters? It is enthralling. What a fantastic number he must have written.

I shall not read about dear Queen Mary, who (oddly?) does not interest me, any more than her second-rate son (eldest) did. She and the bearded saint, as Roger called him, must have been very indifferent parents. But much may be forgiven him for (a) when asked what film he would like to see when convalescing, answering 'Anything except that damned Mouse' and (b) when the footman, bringing in the early morning royal tea, tripped and fell with his load and heard from the pillow 'That's right; break up the whole bloody palace'. The old autocratic touch.

14 November 1959   *Bromsden Farm*

I've decided that I prefer writing on Saturday when I can: there's less pressure of time, and I can still nourish the comforting illusion that all my publishing work can be done on Sunday. This week I also have to draft a 'press release' about the new Phoenix Trust[1], of which (unless my draft is unprintable) you should read something in the papers during the next fortnight. And I must compose a speech for Jonathan Cape's eightieth birthday dinner on Monday. I inadvertently misled you about that broadcast, which was in fact this afternoon, but you didn't miss much, and I am still recoiling from the horror of hearing in cold blood what my daughter assures me is my

[1] For the origins and objects of this Trust, see volume three of these letters.

own voice—ugh! My *coup* of the week was to persuade Winston (through his wife) to write to *The Times* about the London Library. I expect you saw his letter this morning. I only hope it brings in a few more cheques: so far we've had upwards of £3500, and there's a long way to go. Alan Pryce-Jones wrote an article for *The Times's* Thursday book-page (where he operates as George Cloyne—what a name to choose!), but the editor said the Library had been given enough space —two brief letters and a tiny leader! So now I'm trying to get the article on to the back page of the *Lit. Supp.* I very much missed our monthly crack in Soho Square, but thank goodness I caught you in time to prevent your standing impotently on the rainswept pavement with the handle of your favourite bell adrift in your hand.

It's really high time Cuthbert was mercifully put away: he's a misery to himself and a ghastly nuisance to everyone else. When he left he was still complaining that 'the whole atmosphere of the club has changed' (if he hates it, why not resign?), and when he claimed to have lost his hat and coat (with the strong implication that they had been deliberately stolen) I slipped quietly out into the night. Roger was charming at dinner, and so was Andrew Devonshire. Before dinner Cuthbert asked Brand: 'What claim has the Duke of Devonshire to belong to the *Literary* Society?' To which Brand mildly replied: 'About as much as I have', which temporarily shut the old curmudgeon up. I thought Jonah looked very ill, but he rang up next day to explain that he was perfectly well except for his breathlessness, but breath seems to me rather an important thing.

You're clearly much fussier about your food than I am. I positively like all your *bêtes noires*, except pike and whale, which I've never consciously eaten and certainly don't yearn for. I think the only things I positively dislike are brains, tripe, black pudding, trotters, hearts and a few other varieties of so-called edible offal. I always avoid fish with lots of little bones, and remember with sympathy the entry in an old book of etiquette about eating game, which began: 'Tantalising though these small birds may be . . .'

I read the Druon trilogy twice—once in French and once to correct the translator's worst howlers—and I still think it jolly good. What about that blind old man following the staghunt on his relief map— and his later marriage to his old mistress?

I'm sure you *will* read *Lolita*, but you will be bored and disgusted, so now you know!

Middleton Murry I only *just* knew, when Cape was his publisher and I was there. As a man he was a weak and pathetic mess, but as a *literary* critic he was often very good—on Keats, Shakespeare and Swift, for instance.

Too bad about your Pooterish trousers, and I loved the story of the joke played on T. Talbot. Some of my clothes are certainly old enough to split, but none have yet.

The only joke I've so far collected for my speech is this:

PATIENT: 'I can't think what's the matter with me these days, Doctor. I can't remember a thing.'

DOCTOR: 'Dear, dear, when did this start?'

PATIENT: 'When did *what* start?'

I expect you heard it at your prep-school, but it'll have to do for Monday, *faute de mieux*. I'm also told that the latest popular game in America is called Incest—all the family can join in! As they say these days, how funny can you get?

My bird-table is back in action, and the nuthatches seem ravenous. Also I surprised a green woodpecker in the garden today. When, as I hope, you pay us your Christmas visit, you will find the library transmogrified by the introduction of new curtains and chair-covers—its first ever, since the old ones were bought for our London house well over twenty years ago, and were hanging in strips like old flags in military chapels.

The penultimate batch of Oscar photostats arrived from America last week, and Ruth and I are busily grappling with them. The book is getting bigger and richer steadily. What shall I do without it? The answer is the thousand and one other things I ought to be doing now.

18 November 1959   *Grundisburgh*

Yes, Sir Cuthbert in the matter of geniality, tolerance, broad-mindedness, and even ordinary understanding, is *not* improving—at least judging by what he says. But I suppose the fact that he does come shows that he hates and despises us less than he pretends.

I don't think *The Times* has really done you very well about the London Library. A tiny leader, and surely it was lumpish to put Winston's letter in small print. You will get the money surely. Let some U.S.A. tycoon immortalise himself. Why not that ridiculous Getty whose capital I read is 700 million? I suppose he has twenty cars and a thousand shirts.

I enjoyed my London spell, but found it rather tiring. Highgate village *is* a long way off, and a journey underground with perhaps two changes (and what a lot of walking one can do underground!) then a mile in a bus, and ending with a 440 yards walk aren't all that fun. I had a pleasant dinner at Gerald Kelly's one night—he knows almost as many people as you do. For one evening, at any rate, he is good company. I sat next to a nice Russian lady, wife to a genial American whose friends range between Stalin and my Humphrey. He said Stalin's Russian was abominable—worse than the worst Cockney.

I love your story of the man who lost his memory—and laughed out loud when alone, which is the ultimate test of funniness (P.G. Wodehouse passes it repeatedly). And the new American parlour game went down well at lunch in the Ipswich club yesterday.

Pamela returns tomorrow from staying with Roger and wife. My youngest daughter has arrived safely from Malaya and is with a sister at Eton. Her three children demanded to be taken back to Malaya, on the intelligible grounds that England in mid-November was the foulest thing they had struck. To explain to them that to have no snakes, scorpions, tarantulas, sleepy sickness or Malayans constitutes a definite 'bull' point has so far had no success. Of course it would be about eight degrees colder every day than a normal November. I am writing at 3.50 and it is almost pitch-dark. And the shortest day is over a month away. Bah!

Next day. P. has returned from Barbon. She reports that Roger also thought that of course Winston's letter should have been in big print —and the first letter too in the chief column. Will, won't, the Government do something about these exorbitant rates? I see Dr Barnardo's homes are being squeezed now. Damn all jacks-in-office. Also back-benchers who worry mainly about flogging and TV. The coming years are going to be a great test of Macmillan, who must wage ceaseless war against his own Philistines in Parliament and Press. What *would* old Carlyle have said about the squalor and selfishness and stupidity of 1959, seeing how fiercely he attacked those of a hundred years ago? I have been re-reading in Froude's *Life* at meals and found any number of good things. What he called 'men's cussed ways of going on' really did make him miserable—helped no doubt by dyspepsia, but quite obviously genuine. But, as he more than once said, he wasn't always being murdered when he cried out. And after all he did live eighty-five years, before he began 'twinkling away' after longing for his *Dimittis* ever since Jane died. Ruskin's summing-up always strikes me as good. 'What can you say of Thomas Carlyle but that he was born in the clouds and struck by lightning?' Like Johnson it must have been fun to listen to his talk, provided that you carefully refrained from crossing swords.

22 *November 1959*   *Bromsden Farm*

Once again I have been forced by circumstances to retreat to Sunday writing. On Monday I duly delivered my speech after Jonathan Cape's eightieth birthday dinner: there were no others, so I can safely say mine was the speech of the evening. Anyhow it seemed to please the old buzzard and his assembled friends, and thank God it's over. On Tuesday I heard that Hugh Walpole's sister Dorothy had died suddenly of a heart attack in Edinburgh, where at the age of seventy-two she was still practising as a doctor. I am one of her executors, so on Thursday afternoon I travelled north (comfortably reading in a first-class Pullman) and stayed the night with my co-executor, a nice intelligent fortyish Edinburgh lawyer (W.S.). Dorothy, bless her, left me £1000, which will safely cover the rest of Adam's Eton bills, and so relieve me of a perpetual headache. I don't think I've ever bothered you with my financial worries, but in fact I haven't (never have had) a penny of capital, and since my income is only just enough for our modest expenses, all school-fees have always had to be conjured out of the air. Somehow we have struggled on from half to half (once it was almost Long Leave before I got the money) and a week ago the total in my reserve (school-fees) account was £125—not enough for the next Eton bill, and I have also to find £200+ a year for Duff. So you can imagine what a blessing this legacy is. Also, when Robin, the surviving brother, dies, all Hugh's copyrights and royalties (if there still are any) are to belong to me. Robin is sixty-seven and so simple as to be scarcely capable of looking after himself. He has lived with Dorothy for the past ten years and she looked after him. Now I fear my co-executor will have to bear the brunt. Dorothy was deeply religious (their father, you remember, was Bishop of Edinburgh) and on Friday I attended *three* services (all in the rain)—one at the little church she went to, one at the crematorium, and one at the burial of the ashes in a charming country churchyard at Dalmahoy, where the parents are buried. A delightful old Scotch canon conducted all three, reading and speaking beautifully, and the Bishop of Edinburgh gave a goodish address at the first one. He ended with this prayer, which I had never heard before:

> Go forth upon thy journey from this world, O Christian soul,
> In the name of God the Father Almighty who created thee,
> In the name of Jesus Christ who suffered for thee,
> In the name of the Holy Ghost who strengtheneth thee,
> In communion with the blessed Saints, and aided by Angels and
>   Archangels and all the armies of the heavenly host.
> May thy portion this day be in peace, and thy dwelling the
>   heavenly Jerusalem.

Very beautiful, don't you think? I later copied it from the Scottish Prayer Book, where it appears under 'The Visitation of the Sick', though the Canon told me it is seldom so used, since its recitation doesn't exactly encourage the sick person.

After spending the rest of the day with Robin, and trying to explain everything to him, I caught the 10.50 p.m. train, on which I had booked a sleeper, and got to London fairly exhausted yesterday morning—and so down here, where I have slept a good deal.

The London Library has now received close on £5000, and there seems a good chance of Christie's holding a special sale on the Library's behalf. T.S.E. gets back next week.

I lived at Highgate for some years, but wouldn't do so again. Either right *in* London (over the shop in Soho Square) or right in the country, I should say, unless one has cars and chauffeurs.

The final batch of Oscar letters arrived from America last week, but when shall I find time to assimilate them? Tomorrow Ruth and I go to *Rosmersholm*, on which I will report.

Did you see the one-shot serialisation of my Dickens book in to-day's *Sunday Times*? They paid £500 for it (£450 to the author, £50 to R.H-D. Ltd) and I hope the publicity will sell out the first edition. Your copy shall go to you tomorrow. It comes out next Friday.

Last week we won another dictionary and a 15/- book-token with my crossword solutions. There's nothing like wasting one's time in a profitable way. I've almost finished *Past and Present*, and am inclined, after what you say, to go on to Froude next. Although G.M.Y. had become a nuisance (not to me)

> Men are we, and must grieve when even the shade
> Of that which once was great is passed away.[1]

I am trying to persuade Sparrow to edit a short memorial volume of his letters etc.

25 November 1959   *Grundisburgh*

It 'ails from the prime foundation', as Housman put it about some much lesser wrong, that you should ever be harassed about money. I positively ache with sympathy, because I know how much it would depress me and get between me and anything I was doing—and you never show any signs of it. So I rejoice heartily over the Walpole £1000, and wish it was ten times the size. Don't go and plonk a single penny of it on the London Library. That just cries out for a millionaire with quite ordinary good sense and feeling to put it out of reach of all harm with a scratch of his pen. Odd to me that one hasn't already done so. There must be good Carlyleans in the States in spite of his derisive summing-up of their civil war as a smoky chimney which had caught

[1] Wordsworth, 'On the Extinction of the Venetian Republic'.

fire. I cannot believe you wouldn't enjoy Froude's *Life*, though I cannot remember meeting anyone who finds such rich enjoyment in it as I always have. They just never mention it. There is of course too much groaning and grousing, which is not easy to skip, though desirable, because brilliant flashes may lighten the darkness at any moment, and no one could relish them more than you will. You keep on coming across things like the juryman who stuck out against the other eleven, his head 'all cheeks, jaw, and no brow, of shape somewhat like a great ball of putty dropped from a height'; on Margaret Fuller, 'a strange lilting, lean old maid, not nearly such a bore as I expected.' There is any amount of his grisly laughter. Meanwhile I note that the sympathy and conviction that the London Library must be saved is unanimous and growing. The law is much less rigid than it used to be about wills, and clearly should be about rates levied on institutions like the L.L. and Dr Barnardo's homes.

I was sorry to see G.M. Young's death, though I didn't know him except through those *first-rate* little books that were about the first of your fairy-gifts to me. A big batch of extracts from his observations on men and things found their way into my commonplace book and from that to my Governor-General nephew in N.Z. who uses them in his speeches (which recently were called in a N.Z. paper the best ever made by a N.Z. Governor-General!). I can well believe it, as they (G.M.Y.) are never commonplace or platitudinous, and platitude is the occupational disease of G.-G.'s.

I *say*, Rupert, *The Curtain Falls*!! I finished it nicely balanced between fascination and horror. *Superb* descriptions, but what frightful people, and the author's disgust and pleasure in depicting the loathsomeness of the human body, male and female, especially of the old, and his almost gloating over their dreadful deaths is positively Swiftian. Was the degradation of inter-war France really as bad as that? And do tell me what did/do the French think about the book? It surely is an appalling picture, no other word for it. I literally could not put it down. The reviews I have seen don't seem to realise the size and strength of Druon, do they?

Very busy today. New car arrived, and Pamela was shown the ropes. She will have to get used, by trial and error, to the brake and the accelerator having changed places, which no doubt is as it should

be, but error might be costly. Then P. had to cook lunch for our Bishop against time. At 1.20 no Bishop. I rang him up, and in words stifled by compunction and the bread and cheese of his own lunch he explained that his secretary for the first time in donkey's years had made a muddle. Extending forgiveness to a Bishop is a luxurious experience. Have you ever had it? And on the top of it I ate his lordship's lunch, so all ended on a happy note.

I have been reading in bed Evelyn Waugh's life of R.A. Knox with ambiguous feelings—as one has, or I do, in reading about Newman. Does God want all that endless heart-searching about Him and how to worship Him? I am a thousand miles away from understanding what those profound minds are at in their ceaseless meditations on such matters.

There is a lovely blunder in the index. Was Bishop G.A. Selwyn laughed into oblivion before your Eton day? He used to be rammed down our throats by visiting preachers as the perfect model all Etonians should copy? I fancy R.A.K. and Co. may have laughed him out of court, and the Headmaster would warn preachers not to mention him. Well, he is mentioned in the pages dealing with R.A.K.'s schooldays. The index has 'G.A. Selwyn (eighteenth-century wit)'. They mixed him up with the other George Augustus who was sacked from Oxford for blasphemy, and spent his time attending executions, visiting morgues and being mildly (and generally indecently) witty. How R.A.K. himself would have enjoyed this supremely rich gaffe!

28 *November 1959*   *Bromsden Farm*

An American visitor this week produced the ultimate Yellow Press headline: it runs: TEEN-AGE DOG-LOVING DOCTOR-PRIEST IN SEX-CHANGE MERCY-DASH TO PALACE.

A complicated story, you may think, but no more involved, I assure you, than my life has been since I last wrote to you. Monday was all right—a normally busy day, ending with an enjoyable evening watching Peggy Ashcroft's lovely acting in *Rosmersholm*—and on Tuesday the trouble began. We were slowly preparing the press-release of the Phoenix Trust to be put out early in December, when the *Evening Standard* (goodness knows how) got the whole story. I refused to tell them anything, but on Wednesday they printed two long and accurate paragraphs about the scheme, and immediately the other papers were round me like a swarm of hornets. To avoid antagonising them all I was forced to rush out an official statement in a couple of hours. Almost all the other Trustees were unobtainable, so I had to get the statement into final form, duplicated, and sent round by hand with covering letters to seven newspapers and press agencies. I daresay you saw it in Thursday's *Times*. That afternoon, while I was being interviewed by a young lady from the *Sunday Times*, the secretary of the Pilgrim Trust (Lord Kilmaine) rang up in a towering rage to say I had no business to say the Phoenix Trust had been 'founded and endowed' by the 'Pilgrim', since all they had done was to lend their name, give us £500 and nominate a Trustee. He calmed down a little when I pointed out that the offending words were the ones from his own Charter which he had read out to me as the Pilgrim T's authority for helping us, but I had to agree to send out a correction, again by hand, to the same seven places. Next morning (Friday) appeared that savagely malicious leader pouring scorn and ridicule on the new Trust. It seems, don't you agree?, an extraordinary thing for *The Times* so to attack a philanthropic scheme directly it's announced, and I can only imagine that the article was inspired, if not written, by some tight-fisted and self-important person (probably a publisher) who fears his pocket may be endangered. I felt the article must be answered, and I drafted a letter, which I hope they will print on Monday. A.P. Herbert was most helpful with telephonic advice. Meanwhile I had to stay up last night to appear (or rather be audible) for eight minutes on the Home Service, talking about the Phoenix Trust. I don't suppose you heard it. Pretty dull, I fear: I only hope comprehensible. The worst thing about such jobs is the time they take: for those eight minutes I was in Broadcasting House for just on two and a half hours! This morning I had to find someone to type my *Times* letter, take it myself in a taxi to Printing House Square and dash to Paddington. You can imagine how much literary or publishing work I have done this week. Though by using *three* secretaries I managed to keep almost abreast of my correspondence. And in the middle of everything I got a cable to say that the wealthy Bollingen Foundation of New York has agreed to finance a multi-volume complete edition of Coleridge's works, for which I've been scheming for several years.

Ruth has been a tower of strength and devotion all the time, bless her.

T.S.E. is back in England and we are to meet to discuss the L.L., on whose behalf I am laying traps for tycoons.

The Duchess of Kent has agreed to present the Duff Cooper Prize on December 17.

So glad you couldn't put down *The Curtain Falls*: the French loved it, and the first volume was awarded the Prix Goncourt.

Just now I took down Cobbett's *English Grammar* for fun: I have the second edition (1824), in which are bound advertisements of all Cobbett's books, obviously written by him. Of the *E.G.* he writes: 'This work has been published to the amount of *fifty-five thousand copies*, without ever having been mentioned by the old shuffling bribed sots, called Reviewers.' That's the stuff! I must read him again. Take care of yourself in London, and don't go near Regent Street after dark. Forgive this hurried letter: I simply *must* read some manuscripts.

St Andrew's Day 1959   *67 Chelsea Square*

But they tell me you *are* coming on Thursday, and if that is so I will spare you a letter. I like to see you in large print and the chief place in to-day's *Times*—where Winston's letter about the London Library should have been. There is no whirlpool of which you are not the centre.

I shall be coming to the Lit. Soc., but I will *not* sit next to the old death'sheadlam twice running. How nice it will be to see you on Thursday.

5 December 1959   *Bromsden Farm*

Paris was worth a Mass, said Henry of Navarre, and surely two postcards are worth a half-length letter. It was angelic of you to bring

171

back my umbrella, and I'm only sorry that I missed you. I remember Hugh Walpole saying of Clemence Dane: 'If that woman leaves her umbrella in my flat *once more* I shall murder her'. So I mustn't do it again. I thoroughly enjoyed my evening, and rejoiced to see you and Pamela looking so well, not to mention the radiantly lovely Diana.

Comfort suggests your coming to lunch on the Sunday, 27 December. Let me know on Tuesday if it suits. It might be as well if you telephoned to Soho Square on Tuesday morning to make sure that Ruth will be there at 6 to let you in if I am kept at my meeting. She has every intention of being, but I don't want to chase you across London as I did last month. I shall think of you on Monday night, beaming benevolent and Chips-like at Old Boys whose names you can't quite remember—or are there none such?

The Phoenix Trust is attacked again this morning, by a disgruntled and professionally agin-the-Government author. I hope someone will answer, and so keep the controversy alive. R.A. Butler was very sympathetic to the London Library when I saw him last week at lunch at the Birkenheads'. We discussed the Dilke case, and when he admitted that Joe Chamberlain probably did nothing to prevent D's disgrace and disappearance, I said: 'It's a dirty game, politics'. 'Yes', he answered simply; 'You see, it's for power.' He struck me as immensely self-satisfied, but fundamentally right-minded. His new wife is most charming and easy to talk to.

Adam, though nothing like as good at games as Duff, seems to have the valuable gift of being on the winning side: after his winning captaincy in the Junior Soccer League and Junior Cricket, he has now been in the side which last week won the Second Fives cup for Fred's. Adam says the cup is hideous, but honour is satisfied. Duff returns from Oxford tomorrow, so there is much cooking to be done. I have brought down a great chunk of Oscar, having decided that he must be despatched to the printer before Christmas, finished or unfinished.

Diana Cooper looked in on Friday: she is spending the week-end at Petworth, where the P.M. is shooting. Diana is determined to make him take action about the London Library.

Tuesday was even better than usual—beginning with the lovely vision of Ruth at the foot of the stairs and ending, if you please, with a long and good crack with Roger, Ivor B., and Jonah till 11.30, all three in excellent form. Earlier in the evening your ears should have tingled, for your heroic work for the London Library is seeping into the consciousness of men, as of course it should and must. And as your reward you had old Cuthbert to yourself with no relief from his other side! I hope those who say they are coming and then don't have to pay up? It is bad clubmanship. We shall have none of poor old Jonah till the summer, as he tells me he has been ordered abroad for his chest—Portugal I think—for the next four months. What will Cuthbert say about that? I suppose the leeches know what they are doing.

On Friday I take the chair at a village brains-trust. The first question sent in is 'Would you in the next world prefer to be a dog, a cat, or a budgerigar?' I suppose you know the right curtailed pronunciation of budgerigar on the Cholmondeley = Chumley principle? Three guesses.

Love to R. Would she or you object if I said she was a darling? *Yes.* So I won't (but she is all the same).

Cuthbert was much less disagreeable on Tuesday, but he's not exactly a life-enhancer. Gerry Wellington wrote and apologised for not turning up, and Jo Grimond telephoned during the dinner, but Harold N. simply failed to turn up. It's Cyprus that is to harbour Jonah—perhaps they'll elect him President!

Next morning Ruth said: 'There's only one word for George—lovable.' I could think of a few others, but I let it pass.

The best news is (1) Adam has won the Chess Cup—not only the biggest in the school, but apparently bringing with it a fiver in cash! (2) I think I have succeeded in wheedling £1000 for the London Library out of the B.B.C.! But mum is very much the word until the news is official. Privately they asked whether we would mind publicity about the gift. I said on the contrary: it might stimulate other donors. That would bring the total to £6500. Meanwhile the Christie's sale goes forward, and Henry Moore has promised to give a small bronze, which should bring in a few hundred pounds. Soon I must tackle goodness knows how many other possible benefactors. It's a job to know what to do first.

In an attempt to polish off Oscar I brought down an almost unliftable suitcase containing two complete copies of the manuscript, with many attendant books and papers. I've worked on it almost all day, but there's still a helluva lot left to do.

Have you read the Dickens book yet? On Wednesday one of the author's main pieces of evidence was blown sky-high by a Cambridge don, and I had to spend most of that day sorting things out. You'll probably see a couple of letters in tomorrow's *Sunday Times*. Undeterred, the Critics are going to discuss the book *next* Sunday on the radio.

On Wednesday evening I took the Librarian of the London Library to dine in the House of Commons with Leslie Hale, the Labour M.P. who is going to organise a deputation of the thirty-six M.P.s who are members of the Library. He's a vigorous, frank and engaging fellow— a country solicitor from Leicestershire, who has the reputation of speaking faster than any other M.P. In fact they say he can make a speech in the middle of Mr Paget's speech (he's the slowest of all). Unfortunately our host had ordered a mass of wine (sherry, white, red), and it was all opened and decanted, so I simply had to ignore my teetotalism and drink it. A nasty headache all next day seems to prove that I should still keep off it.

After dinner it transpired that the Librarian had never been in the House before, so I asked Hale to give us two tickets for the Strangers' Gallery, where we spent a very dull hour listening to Mr Maudling fluently spouting about Unemployment to a largely empty chamber. Fancy spending one's working life there—ugh!

I was most touched by Roger's kind words at the London Library. Most of the committee are like lumps of driftwood, moving sluggishly with the current, so R's intervention was as unexpected as it was encouraging, bless him.

Duff has got another story (a short amusing one) in the Christmas number of *Argosy*. He has developed a painful boil on his leg and has spent today in bed, very sorry for himself. I think they'll all three be here at Christmas: let me know if the Sunday's okay.

Diana Cooper has sent me most of her third volume—in the roughest form—and I shall have to spend some of the Christmas holiday trying to get it into preliminary shape. Her servant-problems at Chantilly would make a book of their own: she's had dozens of every age, sex and colour—Chinks, Philipinos, West Indians, French, Italian, English. A pair of refugee Poles, who arrived penniless on a tandem bicycle, left two years later with a three-ton lorry full of loot. They went back to Poland, but didn't like it, and came back the other day. Diana said they could inhabit the lodge as soon as the sacked French gardener left. He now refuses to budge, and the Poles are squatting querulously on the top floor of the house. Meanwhile the Algerian cook, who was sacked last week for striking Diana's French maid ('*il m'a giflé!*'), was murdered next day by another Algerian. Never a dull moment! Next week Diana is coming over for the presentation of the Duff Cooper Prize, which this year is being given by the Duchess of Kent to Paddy Leigh Fermor for his book *Mani*, a large tome about southern Greece. Ruth and I have had to arrange everything and send out all the invitations. Diana's list was written in pencil, all names spelt wrong and no addresses.

She tells me that last week-end at Petworth she gave the P.M. a memorandum about the London Library (I'd love to have seen it) and he seemed most sympathetic and interested—as I'm sure he is. One can't have too many irons in this particular fire.

All the same, I wish I was with Ruth in Kisdon Lodge, reading another chapter of *How Green* by the open range! June seems a long way away.

> It is not many miles to Mantua?
> No further than the end of this mad world.

I bet you don't know where that comes from!

This weak utterance comes to you so to speak *de profundis*. Not that I have been seized with 'intestine stone or ulcer, colic pangs' or any species of 'wide-wasting pestilence,' but simply because I have to deal with a large batch of scripts by a monstrous regiment of young women. The questions are on 'Narrative Poems of To-day' and to every question the young women write, in that horrid looping, swooping hand so many of them affect, voluminously, never quite on or off the point, enthusiastically, insipidly. The after-effects are what you get from immersion in a very large bath, quite full of luke-warm water, and I recall Arnold Bennett's recipe for the right treatment of Mrs Humphry Ward's heroines, i.e. that they should be gathered in a besieged city about to fall, all armed with revolvers to protect them from the cruel and licentious soldiery, that the city falls, the soldiers burst in—and all the revolvers turn out to be unloaded.

I see the M.C.C. has followed the L.L. down the rates-drain—and I doubt if M.C.C. has an R.H-D to salvage them. *The Times* strikes the right note of angry contempt for the framers of this degraded law.

Please congratulate Adam from me on his Chess Cup. Yes I remember it—far the largest. But there was no cash with it in my day. Not that I ever won it. I was in the final, *aetat* eleven, at my prep-school, lost, and burst into tears. How often one is *very* unhappy at the age of ten. And on the whole what hateful places prep-schools, anyhow, were, especially if situated, as mine was, among the brickfields near Uxbridge.

Your Oscar saga is really enthralling. You could make a grand production by simply telling your experiences while compiling it, incidentally pillorying that morose and curmudgeonly old b-tch you told me about. It must surely be a best-seller.

I am sorry about your still being on the waggon. Your jaundice was aeons ago. Are you sure it wasn't D.T. or cirrhosis of the liver? Doctors can be very tactful. And there goes old Winston, positively pickled in alcohol, and never having an ache or pain. All men are *not* equal.

The servant problem really is—! Yesterday we lunched with the Bishop. He opened the door, carved and handed round everything and whisked the joint out to, I think, the gardener. Diana Cooper's experiences are thrilling. We haven't yet got to cooks killing each other.

Your Mantua quotation beats me. Whence is it? I forget more and more, quicker and quicker.

19 December 1959   Bromsden Farm

This brief note is not to be answered till *after* your visit here—and in the meantime a Christmas truce or moratorium will prevail. I have been working all day at Oscar (on Monday he goes to the printer) and am so sleepy and cloth-headed that I think I'd better go to bed and write more in the morning. I'm reading *Coningsby* in bed and so far enjoying it greatly.

Sunday morning—rain, gale and all.

I wanted to write a brief footnote about *Coningsby*, and the simplest way seemed to be to read the book—footnote-hunting is now my only excuse for reading anything decent. When I was at Eton we were given *Sybil* for a holiday-task, and I was surprised at how much I liked it. So far I have read only the Eton section of *C*, and will report further next week.

Adam got another Distinction in Trials (his fifth), but missed the Trials Prize by nineteen marks, his conqueror being a lad named Motley, whom he beat in the final of the Chess Cup.

The best news is that the B.B.C.'s cheque for £1000 reached the London Library last week, with a very nice letter from Sir Ian Jacob. This I hope to use as a lever to prise open the coffers of ITV. Also, to my great surprise, the *New Statesman* responded to my appeal with a cheque for £250! The Library has now received £7000 in all, and I am pressing on. The Phoenix Trust will just have to wait. Like the man pursued by the Hound of Heaven, I feel 'trellised with inter-twining charities'.

The presentation of the Duff Cooper Prize went off well. Evelyn Waugh (who has promised a manuscript for the Christie sale) is now very fat, glassy-eyed, and carries an ear-trumpet! I told him it suited him and he should never be without it.

I saw S.C. Roberts for a moment at the Jepsons', benign and charming as ever. Those two lines about Mantua were written by Maurice Baring, and you're supposed to think they come from *Romeo and Juliet* —which indeed they might.

I still haven't got a single Christmas present, so my next few days will be busy. I shall think of you in the midst of your progeny, taking credit for all the individual presents that Pamela has so cleverly bought. Have a nice time, and turn up here some time before one on Sunday. I think the whole family will be here to greet you.

Now I must tidy up Oscar for his journey.

New Year's Eve 1959   *Cambridge*

H.K. Marsden motored me here on Monday—the dullest drive in England variegated by H.K.M.'s jumpy nerves. Once he braked so suddenly that the car behind gave his a kick in the pants; he didn't even get out to look, but sourly assumed it was the bumper.

I dined with old Gow who was in fair form considering he was the next morning to have a wisdom tooth out, which the leech said the X-ray *might* show to be 'impacted', i.e. grown into all the surrounding bones and only separable with a hatchet under chloroform in a nursing home. In old days I suppose one just mildly died of phossy jaw (spelling?).

Last night we went to a film—*Great Expectations*. Excellent. All the setting and scenery etc were masterly. Mrs Gargery was made too savage. She didn't merely give Pip a cut or two with 'Tickler' but *thrashed* him, thereby making one despise Joe, who stood by doing nothing. Joe irritates me in fact in both book and film.

I suggest *Sybil* is really a much better book than *Coningsby*, but it is decades since I read either.

A don here told us—not knowing I knew you—that 'Hart-Davis was doing wonders about raising money for the London Library.' I didn't contradict him!

Yesterday I was given a lovely Penguin, *Yet More Comic and Curious Verse*. An excellent volume—full of things I had never seen or heard of, though of course you have. You won't mind being reminded of the couplet:

> God in his wisdom made the fly,
> And then forgot to tell us why.

We are off to another film this evening, I don't know what, but they swear it isn't rubbish. I'll believe it when I see it. Last night I was smoking one of Alexander's cigars, and the slightly bibulous attendant exclaimed 'Lummy, here come the millionaires'. Just the effect we were aiming at!

INDEX